Kateri Tekakwitha
The Lily of the Mohawks

written and illustrated by
Lillian M. Fisher

D0064081

Pauline
BOOKS & MEDIA
BOSTON

Library of Congress Cataloging-in-Publication Data

Fisher, Lillian M.
    Kateri Tekakwitha : the lily of the Mohawks / written and
illustrated by Lillian M. Fisher.
        p.   cm.
    Includes bibliographical references.
    ISBN 0-8198-4201-X (paperback)
    1. Tekakwitha, Kateri, 1656-1680. 2. Mohawk women—
Biography. 3. Mohawk Indians—Religion. 4. Blessed—New York
(State)—Biography. I. Title.
E99.M8T458   1995
974.7'004975—dc20
[B]
                                                    95-37617
                                                    CIP

Printed and published in the U.S.A. by Pauline Books & Media,
50 Saint Pauls Avenue, Boston MA 02130-3491.

http://www.pauline.org

Pauline Books & Media is the publishing house of the Daughters
of St. Paul, an international congregation of women religious
serving the Church with the communications media.

2 3 4 5 6 7   03 02 01 00 99 98

Contents

About the Author 5

Chapter One 7

Chapter Two 10

Chapter Three 17

Chapter Four 22

Chapter Five 29

Chapter Six 38

Chapter Seven 44

Chapter Eight 52

Chapter Nine 57

Chapter Ten 66

Chapter Eleven 72

Chapter Twelve 79

Chapter Thirteen 84

Chapter Fourteen 91

Chapter Fifteen 98

Chapter Sixteen 105

Chapter Seventeen 112

Chapter Eighteen 115

Author's Note 121

Bibliography 123

Glossary 124

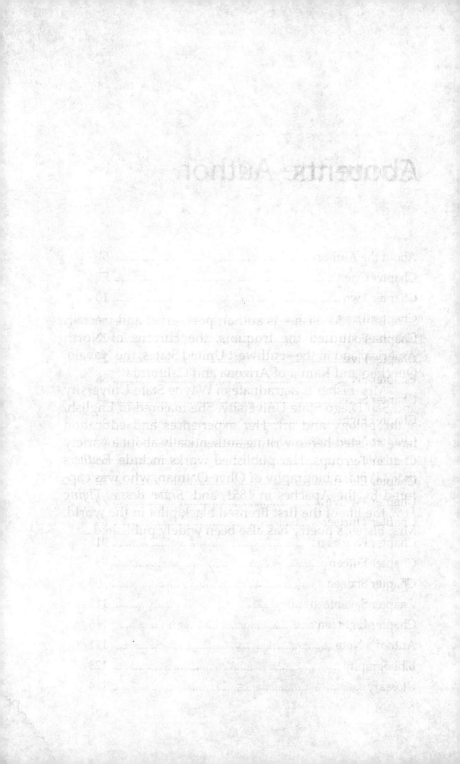

About the Author

Lillian M. Fisher is author, poet, artist and teacher. She has studied the Iroquois, the Hurons of North America, and in the southwest United States, the Navajo, Quechen and Kamia of Arizona and California.

Mrs. Fisher is a graduate of Wayne State University and San Diego State University. She majored in English, anthropology and art. Her experiences and education have assisted her in writing authentically about a variety of ethnic groups. Her published works include *Feathers in the Wind*, a biography of Olive Oatman, who was captured by the Apaches in 1851, and *Brave Bessie, Flying Free*, the life of the first licensed black pilot in the world. Mrs. Fisher's poetry has also been widely published.

Chapter One

Two hungry dogs sniffed at the doorway of the long house of Chief Tsaniton-gowa. There had been no sign of activity for days. One of the curs nipped nervously at the heels of the other and snarled. Then he raised his head and whined.

Inside the long house the stench of death was heavy. Empty now were the middle benches, but sleeping shelves that spanned the walls contained the limp or stiffened bodies of dying and dead Mohawks.

Tsaniton-gowa, chief of the Turtle Clan at the village of Ossernenon, turned his face to the wall and breathed his last. His Christian wife, Kahontake, lay nearby, unaware that her husband and her small son, Otsiketa, had died. Her four-year-old daughter, Ioragode, stirred, then moaned and reached for her mother. Weakness overtook her; the smell in the long house made her retch. She leaned over the side of the shelf and relieved herself.

The fire in the center hearths of the lodge had long ago died. The smoke holes in the ceiling breathed in crisp cool air, but not enough to freshen the fetid interior. Again Ioragode called to her mother. No answer came.

The smallpox in 1660 spared few people in the village of Ossernenon. Anastasia, an Algonquin Christian and friend of Kahontake, survived the plague. Now she drew back the skin that covered the doorway of the chief's long house, afraid of what her eyes would see even before she entered the silent dwelling. There in the semi-darkness she saw Kahontake and little Otsiketa beside her, motionless. Nearby Tsaniton-gowa had turned to the wall in the agony of death, his hand, poised as if attempting to strike out at some horrible enemy. Anastasia fell upon her knees and wept, a prayer on her lips. But in the dim stillness she was conscious of a slight movement. A low pitiful moan escaped from the darkness and quickly she got to her feet. Ioragode was alive!

The customary Mohawk burials were set aside in this time of evil. There had been so many deaths, those weakened members who survived placed brothers and sisters on their biers without ceremony. Soon the funerals were over and there was work to be done.

Anastasia pulled the skin from the doorway, letting in clean air. She carried away the soiled furs and burned them. She covered the earthen floor with sweet dried grasses and swept it clean. Fresh furs and blankets lined Ioragode's sleeping shelf and Anastasia brought hot *sagamite* and herb teas and held the child while she fed her. Nothing would erase the scars from the round face of the four-year-old child, but the healing poultice was applied anyway.

In a weak voice Ioragode called for her mother. "I want to see her. I want to talk to her and feel her arms around me," she whimpered.

"Your mother has gone to heaven. She is with the one true God, Little Sunshine. She is not dead. You will see her again one day. The blackrobes brought her the message. Your mother was a Christian the same as I. She will never die."

"But I want her here with me. Now." Ioragode's tears ran down her scarred face and onto her doeskin dress.

Anastasia smoothed the dark hair, parted and plated with colored ribbons. "Shhhh," she soothed. "Little Sunshine, shhhhh. Your mother is happy now."

Ioragode brought her hands to her face. "My face is rough. Am I ugly?"

Anastasia smiled sadly. "The scars, the pock marks will never go away. But you are still beautiful. Your soul is beautiful."

Ioragode sat up. "What is a soul?"

"The soul, Little Sunshine, is that part of you that never dies. The blackrobes say it is so."

"I want to be a Christian like my mother. She told me many times the only way to happiness was through the one true God, *Rawanniio*."

Anastasia turned her head and looked back as if someone might be lurking nearby. She lowered her voice. "Remember this, Little Sunshine. You are a Mohawk and the Mohawks despise Christians. Your father's brother-in-law, Iowerano, will now be chief and tomorrow he will come into this house. He will bring his wife, Karitha, and her sister Arosen. You will have an adopted sister, Enita. They will be your family and you must obey them. Never speak of the blackrobes or of Christians."

Ioragode frowned. "I will obey them. But they shall never know my thoughts."

Anastasia put her arms around Ioragode. "Soon I must go back to my long house. I will pray for you, Little Sunshine. I will ask the blackrobes to pray for you, also."

CHAPTER TWO

Iowerano succeeded Tsaniton-gowa as chief. He brought his family to live in his brother-in-law's long house. He sat Ioragode down on the bench and spoke to her in stern words, yet he patted her hand as if to reassure her.

"Your aunt and I will care for you until you marry, Ioragode. When we are old you and your husband will care for us. You must choose well. A good husband is one who is a good hunter and can provide food for the family. Karitha will do her best to bring you up to be a desirable wife. She will teach you all she knows."

Ioragode swallowed hard, dropped her gaze and stared into the hearth. "I will do my best to be a deserving daughter, Uncle. I already know how to make mats out of corn husks."

Iowerano nodded. "You will be a good daughter, I am certain of that. Your father was a great Mohawk chief."

"My mother was a good Algonquin. I loved her...."

Ioragode fought back the tears. She wanted to be strong.

"The *okis*, the evil spirits, were responsible for her death and that of your father and brother. Now we must move Ossernenon. We will call it Kannawage."

Ioragode looked up quickly. "Move?" she asked. How could she move away from the home she loved?

"It is what we do when the *okis* come," Iowerano said, his face like stone. He got to his feet abruptly, took up his gun and left the long house.

On the new site, two rows of log stockades enclosed an assembly of long houses, some a hundred feet in length, which would house many families. The village was built near the river. The corn fields would be planted along the shore. Karitha said the blackrobes called the Mohawk towns castles or palisades. She was proud. "We are strong Mohawks," she said. "The French, the English...no enemy would dare attack us."

There was a hint of spring in the breeze. A whisper of fine green leaves veiled the trees. The sun seemed brighter, warmer, but Ioragode pulled her blanket tighter. From the hill she watched the flames start, the smoke billow and cloud the blue sky. She watched the long house of her parents swallowed by flames, slowly crumble. She held back tears. Her small body trembled and she looked away. Nothing would be the same now and a loneliness she had never known before took hold of her. The happy life she had known at Ossernenon was lost forever.

The new village was erected not far from the old settlement. Iowerano was certain the stockades would protect the castles. His long house resembled the old one, except it was smaller. Many families had lived in the house of Tsaniton-gowa. A pair of families shared one hearth in the center and in the old house there had been many hearths. The dwelling of Iowerano lodged only the chief's family.

Ioragode's small space contained a sleeping shelf and a bench. Enita made her place on the opposite wall. During the day the house was gloomy and cheerless. Light came from above through a single smoke hole. Windows were not a part of the *gan-a-sotes*, the bark houses, but in good weather the door covering was pulled back to let in light. The new surroundings seemed strange to Ioragode and because her eyesight was poor she kept bumping into things.

Her aunts enjoyed styling and oiling her long thick hair and delighted in adorning her with ribbons and beads. They dressed her in a beaded buckskin tunic and leggings and ornate moccasins.

"You are the daughter of a great chief," Karitha said. "You must dress accordingly." Ioragode showed no desire for finery. She gathered wood for the fire and kept the water jars filled. She obeyed her aunts, always with a smile, and quietly went about her tasks. No one knew of the terrible grief that swelled her heart.

Ioragode's new father was a stranger to her. In the evenings he sat by the fire in stern silence, smoking his long stemmed pipe, staring into the fire as if seeing visions or ghosts. His hair had been shaven on each side of his head and the remaining hair was greased and combed upward like a coxcomb. He wore a necklace of bears' claws and another of wampum—white, purple and striped shell beads. Sometimes Ioragode pretended it was her own father sitting there, looking into the fire. But Iowerano's thin lips were set in a straight line, his expression like stone.

Smallpox may have been the white man's cruel gift to the Indians, but the *okis* had played their evil tricks on Ioragode's eyes. The *shaman*, the tribal medicine man,

danced wildly, whirling and turning in frenzied agitation. He made hideous faces, chanted, burned sacred herbs and shook his rattles, but he could not banish the evil spirits.

Ioragode had been endearingly called Little Sunshine, but now the bright light of the sun gave her pain and she stayed inside the long house for hours at a time. When she did go outdoors to gather wood for the cooking fire, she was forced to shield her eyes with her hands, or pull a blanket over her head to shade her face. She often walked with her arms outstretched, feeling her way along so as not to run into tree stumps or rocks.

One evening Iowerano turned to Ioragode and said, "It is time we bestow your permanent name."

Karitha and Arosen leaned closer. "We have thought of many names," said Arosen. "Each is fitting."

Iowerano watched his stepdaughter closely. "I can think of no better name than 'Tekakwitha.'"

"Yes," said Karitha quickly. "A perfect name. Tek-ak-witha means she pushes with her hands. Ioragode does this."

"It also means one who is industrious and hard working," Arosen chimed in. "She who puts things in order."

"It is done," said Iowerano, turning again to his stepdaughter. "From this moment on, you will be known as Tekakwitha."

Tekakwitha accepted her new name just as she had accepted all the changes in her young life. Cheerfully she went about her chores, gathered wood, brought fresh water, cooked and served meals to the family. Her gentle nature endeared her to everyone.

Winter came again and at night legends were told around the hearth. Tekakwitha listened to the tales of her ancestors with deep attention. The long house was cozy and warm. Iowerano puffed on his pipe while he stared into the fire. Karitha told stories of Hiawatha and his wonderful dreams for the *Ho-de-no-sau-nee*, the Iroquois. Tekakwitha begged to hear more.

"The legend of the great Chief Hiawatha tells us," Karitha said, "that an Iroquois brave had a dream, a dream that gave him great power. The power gave him knowledge to know what was best for his people. It pained him to watch his people at war, tribes fighting tribes, families fighting each other. He wanted them to live in peace with each other and with everyone."

Tekakwitha's eyes grew wide with wonder. "Did he decide to help his people?"

Karitha nodded. "He dressed himself in pure white buckskin and fashioned a canoe of white birch bark. He traveled far, paddling the canoe in clear waters until he came to the place where the great Hiawatha lived."

"What was the brave's name?" Tekakwitha asked, her soft voice filled with excitement.

"His name was Peacemaker."

Tekakwitha smiled. She liked that name.

"Peacemaker and Hiawatha," Karitha continued, "talked far into the night like brothers with a single purpose. They agreed that our people should lay down their arms and live in peace with each other.

"It was decided that all the tribes would be summoned to the tallest pine tree in the forest. There they would lay down their arms and bury them. The five tribes were the Onondagas, the Senecas, the Cayugas, the Oniedas, and the Mohawks, all of them Iroquois. Each tribe sent their chiefs who journeyed to the tallest pine. These chiefs or sachems laid down their bows and arrows and tomahawks and there was peace. The League of the Five Nations was born."

Outside, the wind howled, the smoke from the

hearth fire filled the room. Tekakwitha rubbed her eyes. She frowned. It was a beautiful story, but if it were true she wondered, why did the Iroquois still make war with enemy tribes and even with each other? Why did they trade skins, furs and baskets, to the Dutch at Fort Orange for whiskey and guns that made them evil?

Arosen was quick to see Tekakwitha's bewilderment. "What is it?" she asked. "Do you not like the story? It is true. It is true."

"I love the story," Tekakwitha said softly.

"Then why do you frown?"

"I don't understand why our people no longer live in peace. If they accepted Hiawatha's plan, why do we still fight our enemies?" Sadness marked Tekakwitha's face and she shook her head. "We have forgotten how to be good."

Karitha looked up sharply. "Do not speak that way. We live according to *orenda*." She shrugged. "Just sometimes we forget. Just sometimes. Always it is the whiskey."

"The Dutch at Fort Orange should keep their whiskey. The Great Spirit must be sad to witness such evil."

Karitha's eyes shone with a strange pleasure. "Ah, but you forget. There are two Great Spirits. One good and one evil—*Areskoui*, the evil one, the drinker of blood, the killer of enemies. We please him and give him honor when blood is shed."

Tekakwitha shivered, though she was near the hearth fire. The violence, the killings, the frenzied ceremonies, the debauchery, all were wrong. All were evil. She recalled the words of Anastasia. The belief of the blackrobes was so different. They spoke of peace and love. Hiawatha's message was the very same. Tekakwitha caught her breath. A wave of excitement filled her whole being. She wanted to know more about the blackrobes and their prayers. But she dare not ask questions about Christians in Iowerano's house.

CHAPTER THREE

In the winter of 1666, extreme cold, snow and ice gripped the land where the Mohawk castles raised their snowy heads. Trees cracked and their limbs broke from heavy coatings of ice. Snow piled against the doorways of the long houses and the only tracks in the snow were the marks the Mohawks made themselves. Animals hid deeper in their burrows. Corn that had been stored away for the winter months was almost gone; only seed corn remained. The rivers were frozen over in a frigid grasp. The ice was so thick the people could not chop holes for fishing. Wood for the fires was scarce. Although Tekakwitha searched the forest on snowshoes for twigs and branches, her hands and feet tingled with frost before she was able to bring even a small bundle to the long house of Iowerano.

The French in Quebec, Canada, having grown weary of the unceasing attacks on their settlements, assembled an army under the command of M. De Tracy and made a second attempt to subdue the Iroquois. De Tracy chose this time in devious weather to meet the

Mohawks at their very doors. With an army of a thousand men he succeeded in overpowering the enemy, burning some of their stockaded castles—towns which the Mohawks believed could never be penetrated. The village of Kanawage was not spared. After the smoke cleared a new town was built, this time on a hill on the north side of the Mohawk River and the new village was called Caughnawaga. The Mohawks were now subdued and ready to make a grudging peace with the French, even agreeing to allow a few blackrobes to once again come into their settlements.

Iowerano smoldered with anger. "The League has agreed to let a few of the hated blackrobes come into the land of the Iroquois." He muttered something under his breath that Tekakwitha couldn't hear. She had never seen him so angry and upset.

Iowerano traveled great distances to council meetings, to try to persuade the other sachems that their tradition of warfare should be upheld, but the League did not agree.

When spring came, once again game was abundant. Iowerano spent his frustration in hunting. The long period of deprivation had a dour effect on the morale of the town's people. Karitha's words became sharp whenever she spoke to Tekakwitha.

"You are not bringing enough wood into the long house, Tekakwitha. Your chores are not done properly. I am not pleased. Not pleased."

"Yes, Aunt," Tekakwitha replied. "I will try to do better." Sensing her aunt's deep unhappiness she tried in small ways to do special, thoughtful things to make her stepmother smile.

Once again the Mohawk braves traded furs and pelts to the Dutch at Fort Orange. Once again they brought home guns and whiskey and life went on.

Spring bowed to summer and the warm sun laced the trees with gold. The sun also fell upon the dusky shoulders of the Mohawk braves and the maidens who laughed while they toiled lazily in the corn fields. Again it was time for Iowerano to take his family on an annual fishing trip to Tawonsonta, now known as the Cascades. The seasonal journey would take the chief's family down the Hudson River into the land of the Hollanders. Iowerano would trade furs at Fort Orange and in turn he would provide his household with beads, ribbons, knives, kettles and cloth.

Karitha and Arosen were excited. Even Tekakwitha was curious and anxious to be off. She oiled her dark hair, neatly parted and plaited. A long braid, wound with red ribbon, hung down her back. She took her blanket with her for cool evenings when she would drape it over her shoulders.

As the canoe glided down the river past Fort Orange, Tekakwitha strained to see the settlement. The town was enclosed in walls of upright posts. The sturdy trading post had been built on the outside of the settlement. Tekakwitha's poor vision enabled her to see only the roofs of two story houses that sat side by side in even rows. Mohawk houses were erected here and there with no particular plan. Tekakwitha thought that this arrangement was superior to the Dutch design.

Enita called out, "They wave at us. They salute us!"

Karitha and Arosen smiled, but didn't return the greeting. The canoe glided by so fast the Fort was quickly out of sight. Soon Iowerano was slowing his pace. They were nearing Tawonsonta.

Iowerano secured the canoe and began to construct two little dwellings made of pine branches. Karitha and Arosen covered the frames with moose skins. The little houses would be snug and safe.

"Enita! Tekakwitha!" Karitha called. "Gather the wood for the fire. Bring enough to feed it well. It will take much wood to smoke the fish."

Tekakwitha and Enita went quickly and obediently. Iowerano had already laid his nets below the waterfalls and the traps would soon swell with flapping salmon, trout and perch.

The days that followed were filled with cleaning and cutting the catch. The fish were then hung on racks positioned over a smoldering fire. The smoke would dry and preserve them. Large baskets made of birch bark would store the harvest. Looking forward to the taste of fresh roasted fish made all the tasks seem lighter.

Tekakwitha sat on the shore and looked out over the water at the red sunset and turned to Enita. "The Great Spirit, the maker of all things, gave people the sunset to make their lives beautiful. The Great Spirit and *Rawanniio* must be one and the same God." At once she realized she had spoken in a manner forbidden by Iowerano. She hung her head and pulled her blanket tighter.

Enita looked up, startled. "Tekakwitha!" she said, but that was all.

When darkness came, the family retired to the little houses that smelled of sweet pine boughs. The boughs covered the floor and soft furs made the beds comfortable. Tekakwitha lay awake in the darkness, listening to the night sounds, the lapping of the water against the shore, the hoot of an owl in a nearby tree. She was content knowing that when the fishing trip was ended they would head back to Caughnawaga. Iowerano's family would have a good supply of fish, enough to feed them through the summer months until the corn harvest in the fall.

The canoe was loaded with heavy baskets. There was barely room for the beaver pelts Iowerano would trade to the Dutch. When they arrived at Fort Orange, Iowerano moored the canoe. The women waited while he went into the trading post with his furs.

Enita peered at the strange scene and whispered to Tekakwitha. "The men dress so strangely. Their pants come only to the knees and they wear big silver buckles at their waists."

Tekakwitha smiled shyly, shrouded by her blanket. "What do the women wear?" she asked.

"Oh, the women are in long dresses with ruffles. They have keys and scissors hanging from their belts. You should see them, Tekakwitha. The men are staring at us."

Tekakwitha withdrew further into her blanket. Karitha and Arosen pointed, chatted, and laughed, impatient to learn of the wonderful things Iowerano would win in the trade.

This time Iowerano brought two large brass kettles to Karitha. Inside were ribbons and beads and two red blankets, one for Tekakwitha and one for Enita. Arosen received her share of the beads and a copper bracelet. Iowerano caressed a new musket and set it beside two shiny knives. He never drank to excess, but his breath smelled of whiskey, a bonus from the Dutchmen.

Tekakwitha was always happy to return home. From the hill she could look down upon the ruins of the first village. The burned out posts and remnants of the corn storage bins remained. It was easy to tell where the houses had stood. Black rectangles stained the earth. She knew the spot where she had been born. Her mother, father and Ostesika were buried nearby. She would always feel a closeness to the ghost town that had been Ossernenon.

CHAPTER FOUR

In the forest, near the long house of Iowerano, a little spring bubbled up out of the ground and provided Caughnawaga with water. Tekakwitha loved this place. Violets and jack-in-the-pulpits grew near the peaceful spring. Sometimes squirrels and other small animals came to drink and if Tekakwitha sat very still they would come so close to her that she was able to see them. She enjoyed the special spot best in early morning and in the evening.

Today, on this early summer morning, Tekakwitha leaned against a giant fir tree and sat on a bank of moss. She was alone. Her thoughts dwelled on the "prayer" the blackrobes had given her mother. Kahontake had been baptized. Tekakwitha, too, longed to have the water poured on her head in the sacred ceremony of baptism. Her mother had said, "Happiness comes only through communion with the one true God. I have become one with him. He dwells within my heart. Someday, Little Sunshine, he will dwell within yours."

Tekakwitha kept these words to herself, recalling

them often, treasuring each one, remembering the sound of her mother's voice as she spoke, softly, almost in a whisper as they sat in the corner of the long house.

She heard the snapping of a twig and she sat up quickly, straining to see who it was that came to the spring on heavy feet. As the figure came nearer, Tekakwitha saw that it was Anastasia.

"Tekakwitha," the woman said, "long has it been since I've had a chance to speak with you. Your aunts have kept you at great distance. They think I am a bad influence since I am Algonquin—and a Christian." Tekakwitha's face brightened at the sight of Anastasia. "It is so good to see you. It is true my aunts keep me away from you. I...I must obey."

"I would not want you to disobey them, Tekakwitha, but this is a chance meeting. They will not blame you for this."

Tekakwitha's eyes shone with affection. "I have wanted so many times to go to you. I wanted to speak to you of the blackrobes. I want to learn their ways."

Anastasia shook her head. "Ah, Tekakwitha, I wish it could be so."

Tekakwitha moved closer. "I hear things when I work in the fields. The women talk. It saddens me to think of so much hatred. I wonder, will the Mohawks ever accept the blackrobes?"

Anastasia shook her head and knelt to fill her jar with water, then set it down and settled herself on the bank of moss. "Long before you were born the blackrobes came to bring the word of the white God."

"My mother accepted that word," Tekakwitha said eagerly.

Anastasia nodded. "Yes, but your mother was schooled by the French. She was captured when the Mohawks raided New France. She was an Algonquin slave, but won your father's Mohawk heart with her gentleness and beauty."

"Life must have been painful for her," Tekakwitha said. "She prayed only when no one was there to see."

"Your father knew. He commanded her to pray in private. She would have been punished had the villagers known that she worshipped as a Christian."

"Why do the Mohawks hate the Christians so?" asked Tekakwitha.

Anastasia shrugged her broad shoulders. "Perhaps because they hate the French. When the first Frenchmen came to the land of the Iroquois, they betrayed the trust. They killed many of the chiefs. It is hard to forget, harder to forgive. But then, the Iroquois hate the English, too. They are friends with the Dutch because they like their guns and whiskey."

Tekakwitha bent and moved the water with her hand. It sent little ripples to the edge of the spring. "My heart cries out for the prisoners—those that are tortured and killed at the celebrations."

"The Mohawks offer the sacrifices to *Areskoui*, the god of war, the killer of enemies. That is their religion."

"The Hurons and the Algonquins accepted the message of peace. Why can't the Iroquois do the same?"

Anastasia frowned. "The Iroquois destroyed most of the Huron Nation. They have many enemies. They tortured and killed every blackrobe they could find. They offered the burned flesh of blackrobes to *Areskoui*. The *rakeni* died most cruelly, especially one who called himself Jogues."

"Did you know him?" asked Tekakwitha.

"I was very young, but I remember what happened. The Mohawks tore his heart from his chest, ate his flesh and cut off his head. They placed it on the palisades and they celebrated." Anastasia's eyes clouded with tears.

"There were others, Goupil, Lalemont, De Brebeuf and Garnier."

Tekakwitha shuddered. "I weep for those good men and the *rakeni* who still try so hard to bring peace."

"You will soon meet three of them," said Anastasia.

Tekakwitha's eyes widened with disbelief. "*I* will meet them?"

"The League has made small peace with the French. It has agreed to allow a few blackrobes to come among us as missionaries. Iowerano has no choice. He will do as the council decides. Yes, the blackrobes will come."

Tekakwitha's eyes clouded with fear. "What will Iowerano do?"

"Iowerano will not defy custom. He will house them in his long house even if it turns his stomach to do so."

Tekakwitha brought her hands together. "Oh, Anastasia, how wonderful. When? When will they come?"

"I know not when. I only know that they come. You will be told when your uncle thinks you should know."

Tekakwitha shook her head. "I will say nothing. I will wait."

Tekakwitha filled her water jars and prepared to return to the village. The birds singing in the leafy trees seemed to harmonize with the croaking of frogs. She wanted to stay in the peaceful forest and ask Anastasia many questions, but knowing how Iowerano would view this, she reluctantly left the spring.

In the days that followed, Karitha and Arosen's mysterious whisperings set Tekakwitha to wondering. Enita was given the task of preparing beaver pelts and Tekakwitha was ordered to sweep the long house from one end to the other. When Karitha cooked a stew of dog meat in a large kettle, Tekakwitha suspected that important events were inevitable. Dog meat was a delicacy, served only on special occasions.

Iowerano peered at Tekakwitha, his expression giving no indication of his emotions. He pointed his pipe at her and said, "The blackrobes are coming. You are eleven years old now, old enough to serve guests. It will be your duty to tend to the needs of the *rakeni* for as long as they are in this house. I, for one, will have little to do with them, but they must be treated with hospitality according to what is polite."

Tekakwitha's heart was pounding. She tried to look unconcerned, but she was feeling a whole range of emotions: excitement, shyness, happiness and curiosity. When she turned to leave, her eyes met the narrowed eyes of her aunt.

"Arosen and I," Karitha said, "will make ourselves scarce. I have sent Enita to the long house of her cousin. Tekakwitha will serve the blackrobes food and water. They come as missionaries, but none of Iowerano's family will have need of them."

The stern look in Karitha's eyes revealed her intentions. She was telling Tekakwitha that she must not socialize with the hated *rakeni*.

Iowerano's welcome speech was short, polite and cool. He spoke for his people; he spoke for the council. It was agreed that the blackrobes should be welcomed as missionaries. Father Bruyas, Father Pierron and Father Fremin sat together in full view of the Mohawks. Some of the crowd scowled, no one smiled, all were silent, listening intently to their chief as he grudgingly welcomed the hated blackrobes.

Father Bruyas answered Iowerano, thanking him for the privilege of entering the village. "The true God is the father of all men," he said, his arms folded, his hands hidden in his sleeves. "The red as well as the white. He loves all human beings; and everyone—man, woman and child may speak to him, for he hears every whisper and sees what is in every heart."

Iowerano's stone-like expression spoke more than words. He would cling to his old religion. He wanted no part of the white man's God.

A small space had been cleared in the long house for the three priests and a deer skin hung for privacy. They were given their place on the bench, each was assigned a sleeping shelf. Tekakwitha brought cool fresh water from the spring and served the dog meat with a smile. This was a feast fit for the greatest chief. But Tekakwitha was bewildered by the pained expressions on the faces of the three men. She couldn't understand their hesitation, their seeming reluctance to eat. They smiled at her and politely thanked her, but the amount of time taken to finish the meal was exceedingly long. Shyness swept over Tekakwitha and she bowed her head and turned away. She wondered if the blackrobe's religion demanded that they eat slowly. She knew so little of their customs.

It was getting dark when the meal was finally over. Tekakwitha lit the fire in the hearth and the flames brought the faces of the men into view. The faces were kindly, the voices gentle. Shadows fell upon the walls of the long house and the light from the fire shone upon the silver crosses the blackrobes wore.

"Thank you, my child," said Father Pierron. "May God bless you."

Tekakwitha cleared away the dishes and the three men knelt to pray. She couldn't understand the words, but she sensed they were important and wonderful. They spoke to the one true God.

If only *she* too, knew how to speak to *Rawanniio*, the white man's God. She bounded out the door and into the forest. Father Bruyas said that God knows what is in everyone's heart. Perhaps she didn't need to speak. She remembered the words and whispered them to the silent night. "God hears every whisper. He knows what is in every heart." *Rawanniio* must know of her fervent desire to become a Christian. Perhaps he would help her.

"Great Spirit," she whispered, "I hear your voice in the wind. Sharpen my ears to hear you better. Make my heart pure to know you and my hands ready to do your work. I want to serve you all the rest of my life and I want to serve you as a Christian, my one true God."

CHAPTER FIVE

Father Fremin left for the Tionnaontoge, the Castle of the Bears. Father Bruyas went to the Oneidas. Tekakwitha rejoiced when she learned that Father Pierron would remain at Caughnawaga and share his time at Andagoron, a village not far away.

Quietly she went about her work. Sometimes the women spoke of the blackrobes when they toiled in the fields. Tekakwitha listened and savored every word. She watched when Father Pierron treated the sick with the medicines of the white man. She saw him pour the water upon the heads of the dying infants and make the Christian sign with his fingers.

The *shaman* snarled and spat words of loathing. He shook his rattles, chanted and danced, bared his teeth and made hideous faces. Father Pierron smiled and continued performing his services. He celebrated Mass for the Huron slaves and a few Christian Algonquins. A few Mohawks came to hear his sermons; some even accepted the new faith. But Iowerano remained stiffly aloof and unfriendly, forbidding the members of his family to speak to the *rakeni,* the blackrobe whom he would never forgive for bringing the white God to the Mohawks.

On warm days the door of the bark chapel was left open. Tekakwitha shyly glanced inside as she passed slowly by. She had to force her moccasins to disobey her heart, force them to stay on the worn path that led back to the long house of Iowerano. Sometimes the children sang hymns and she thrilled to hear the music of the white God. She wished with all her heart that she could be part of the Christian community. She longed to worship with the others.

Karitha never ceased to remind her of Iowerano's prejudice toward the *rakeni.* "When you pass the chapel you must hurry. Turn your head. Be loyal to your uncle. Never speak to the Christians."

In the evenings, Iowerano would growl and carry on conversations with himself as he stared into the fire. "The hated blackrobes," he would say, "with their sick smiles and peaceful ways are poisoning the minds of our people. We must be true to our fathers and carry on our traditions. No one in the house of Iowerano will bow to the missionaries and their lies."

Tekakwitha was shy, but she was also afraid of her uncle. Her aunts relentlessly watched her and made certain that she had no contact with the Christians.

Another winter came and left slowly. It was the time of the first thaw and Tekakwitha took her wooden buckets into the forest and fastened them to the maple trees. The sap would begin running any day and she was old enough now to store up maple syrup. It was especially good on *sagamite,* or corn cakes. She even cooked some and made a kind of candy from it. This pleased her aunts.

But as much as she enjoyed watching the flow of the amber sap issue from the trees, she enjoyed her solitude more, there in the quiet forest. Little patches of snow remained here and there and yellow hairs of grass poked up through the icy crusts. The gurgle of a little stream, having been set loose by the turn in the weather, seemed to set the whole world to music. From out of the wet leaves at her feet, a crocus thrust its purple head. Tekakwitha bent and touched it gently with her fingers. The world was awakening.

Here, alone in the forest, she felt the presence of something holy and mysterious. The one true God was here in this quiet place. She was sure. She didn't know as yet how to pray to him, but she believed he could read her thoughts, look into her soul and see how much she loved him. Joy filled her heart and with her knife she carved the symbol of the cross on the surface of a pine tree. She wasn't sure what the cross represented, she only knew the *rakeni* wore one, sometimes carried one. Long ago it seemed, her mother made the sign with her fingers, touching her forehead, her chest, her left shoulder, then her right. Tekakwitha was sure it had a deep meaning. It was a Christian sign and she wanted to be a Christian. She raised the fingers of her right hand to her forehead and made that sign.

Tekakwitha left the forest and hummed all the way back to the long house. She breathed deeply. The air was no longer winter and it was not yet spring, but the air she inhaled was ripe with promise.

In the summer of 1669, Tekakwitha retired to a small hut for seven days, as was the custom when the menses occurred.

"You have come of age, Tekakwitha," Karitha said in a serious voice. "You are now a woman. You are a woman in the house of Iowerano. You must leave your childhood behind you. You must look forward to choosing a mate."

Tekakwitha cringed and pressed her fist to her chest. "I am too young to think of marriage, Aunt. Please don't talk of it. I am content the way things are."

Karitha turned to Arosen with a wry smile. "She shuns the ways of the Mohawk. Could it be that she is more Algonquin than Mohawk?"

Tekakwitha positioned her blanket to cover her forehead. She took up her sewing and followed Enita to the hut which had been especially erected for her.

The small dwelling was dim, but an opening at the top let in enough light to enable her to sew. In the solitude of the special house, she was anxious to stitch the tunic she was fashioning for Enita. She sewed with a needle made from the small ankle bone of a deer. Delicate sinews as fine as thread came from the same animal. She had tanned the skin herself, mixing moss and the brains of the deer to make it soft. Sometimes she used porcupine quills and beads for decorations, arranged in a fashion that told a story. Her wampum belts were especially fine. Iowerano smiled when he saw her handiwork.

The time away from the long house gave Tekakwitha more opportunity to think. She was older now and her desire to be a Christian was becoming a passion. Just how she would accomplish the conversion she didn't know. Iowerano, instead of becoming more tolerant toward the blackrobes, was becoming more hardened. Tekakwitha often feared that he read her thoughts. When he sat before the fire and smoked his pipe in silence, the sternness of his expression laid upon her a guilt which she could not divest.

Karitha aligned herself to her husband's views. "The Huron slaves are stupid Christians," she would say. "The Mohawks should never allow them the choice of another religion. And they should banish Anastasia,

the Algonquin, who knows no better. She is a trouble-maker."

Tekakwitha listened in silence. The words brought pain. She loved Anastasia as she would an aunt. But in the household of Iowerano she could not express her feelings. At times like this she would flee to the forest and kneel beneath the large pine tree with the incised cross. She now had courage to speak to the one true God; she opened her heart to him and believed that he listened. "*Rawanniio*," she whispered, "it is I, Tekakwitha. I am here to serve you, here to love you. Help me to be a better Mohawk who finds a way to also become a Christian." She found great comfort in this act, but her happiness was marred by the fear of discovery.

Iowerano enjoyed hunting. He almost smiled when he brought home a deer or a moose to his family. Karitha praised him and brought him fresh moccasins. Arosen brought his pipe. But the catch meant work and the women toiled all day until the sun disappeared behind the western clouds and turned the sky red. Only then did they enter the long house; only then did they rest.

Weariness overtook Iowerano early in the evening. He was tired from the hunt and now he lay on his shelf in a deep sleep. The women, too, retired, but Tekakwitha found it difficult to sleep. Her heart was heavy with sadness, remembering the words of Karitha.

From the far end of the long house, Iowerano's snoring maintained an uninterrupted rhythm. Looking up at the smoke hole, Tekakwitha saw a star and a patch of bright sky. It was the night of a full moon.

She pulled her blanket about her and taking two empty bark buckets she hurried to the spring. The moon lit her path and she was happy to bring in extra water for the family. Karitha would be pleased.

She returned to the long house and tried to sleep.

Toward morning she was jarred awake. Perhaps it was a pot that had fallen from its place on the wall or perhaps it was the cry of an animal screaming in the clutches of its captive. She sat up. Again silence. Even Iowerano's snoring was softer now.

Suddenly as if the heart of the night had been ripped open by a giant knife, a loud warwhoop rose in the air. Tekakwitha recognized the sound. It was the cry of the Mohicans! Caughnawaga was at once awake and on its feet. Caughnawaga was under attack!

Within moments Iowerano fled from the house with his gun. Then the sound of feet pounded the sand. Soon came the cries of the men as they ran to their posts to protect the stockade. Tekakwitha listened and prayed. Shots rang out and blood-curdling cries. Tekakwitha put her hands to her ears. Anger consumed her, anger that her people caught in a vicious enemy attack would be harmed.

"Oh, Tekakwitha," Karitha said, "the extra water you brought to the long house will help see us through the siege. No one will leave the stockade until the enemy is gone."

Tekakwitha dropped her head further into her blanket and huddled beside the hearth with her aunts and Enita. Outside, the savage cries and gun shots rang out without respite. Tekakwitha prayed, prayed for her people and prayed for her enemies, the Mohicans.

For three long days the siege continued. The kettle that hung over the hearth was empty now, the water jars were dry. The long house was cold and dark, but no one complained. Mohawks had been trained to fast and thirst ever since childhood. It was a way of preparing them for severe trials when endurance meant survival. But the noise from the guns, the screams, the cries of agony, rent Tekakwitha's heart.

On the third day Iowerano entered his long house for the first time since the initial attack. His face bore the blue and red paint of the warrior. His face glistened with sweat, his jaw set in the familiar determined fashion. "We are saved!" he said. "Tionnaontoge received our message. They have come to help. We will defeat the Mohicans. We will destroy them all!"

Arosen drew back the curtain and looked out across the village. "The Mohicans are outnumbered!" she cried. "They have retreated to the woods." Suddenly the silence that followed seemed overwhelming.

Tekakwitha and Enita quickly left the house and joined the other girls. They would tend the wounded and the dying, bringing water and food to those who were stricken.

"Get more water, Tekakwitha," Enita called, "quickly."

As Tekakwitha approached the spring she heard a low moan. A fallen Mohican brave lay in a prone position, his eyes searching the heavens. Tekakwitha brought him a gourd cup of water and poured cool water into his wound. Tears filled her eyes as she looked upon the painted face of the brave. His lips moved in a feeble smile, then the smile faded and his eyes closed in death.

Iowerano returned to the long house and applied fresh paint to his face. He used a small looking-glass he won in a trade at Albany and when he was finished he smiled with satisfaction. He filled his pouches with ground corn and eagerly took up his gun and ammunition.

"Chief Chicattibut, the Mohican, should begin his death song. It is only a question of time and we will find him. Our braves will bring back prisoners and then we will properly celebrate."

Karitha, her broad face shiny in the firelight, said,

"Good luck on the path to war, Iowerano. We will look forward to your return."

Tekakwitha put her hand to her heart. She knew what the celebrations would bring. Methods of torture beyond comprehension, the gnawing of fingers, floggings, the cutting away of flesh, the feasting. Then at the end, the bodies would be encased in bark and set ablaze. She couldn't bear to think of it. Again the tears came.

Karitha pointed a finger. "This time, Tekakwitha, I want you to join in the celebrations. If you are a true Mohawk you will obey *Areskoui*, the killer of enemies. It is his wish that we consume those who do evil against us."

Tekakwitha bowed her head. "Please, Aunt, I wish to stay at home. I will do the work for all of you. I will stitch each of you a most beautiful beaded head band. I do not want to take part in the celebrations."

Arosen smirked. "You are an Algonquin just like your mother. A true Mohawk would take part."

Karitha's half-closed eyes expressed disdain. "One day you will come to your senses. But, all right, stay at home if you wish. Someone needs to do the work."

Tekakwitha sighed with relief. At least for now she would not be forced to watch and take part in the tortures. But already the death songs of Mohican prisoners fell upon the evening. She put her hands to her ears and wept.

Chapter Six

Tekakwitha heard the faint sound of voices raised in song and she hurried to the shore. She brought her hand to her brow, straining to see the canoes bringing the warriors home. Then she saw movement on the river and the voices became stronger, jubilant and victorious. Some of the men held long poles and the scalps of the enemy dangled from the ends. The returning men moored their canoes. Tekakwitha left her hiding place in the cornfields and hurried home.

Iowerano strode into the long house, a crooked smile of satisfaction playing around his mouth where traces of old war paint remained. Weary from the toils of the warpath, he sat down heavily on the reed mat Karitha had prepared for him. She brought fresh moccasins and his pipe and Tekakwitha offered a jar of fresh water. Arosen sat beside the hearth with her arms embracing her knees, waiting eagerly to hear the words of Iowerano.

The chief delayed his speech, as if enjoying the effect his silence had on the women. He puffed on his pipe and the smoke drifted on the air, slowly finding its way to the hole in the ceiling. He took the pipe stem from between his teeth and groaned softly. Arosen moved closer. He opened his mouth as if to speak, sighed and then puffed again on his pipe.

Karitha could stand the suspense no longer. "Tell us," she said breathlessly, "how many prisoners await the celebrations?"

"There are enough to keep everyone busy for three or four days," Iowerano answered. "Chicattibut has been slain by Chief Ganeagowa. Kryn, the brave one, led the battle. The Mohicans were outnumbered and fled, back to their far away home." Again he sighed a mighty sigh, but his weary countenance shone with pleasure.

Tekakwitha withdrew further into her blanket. She knew what the ensuing days would bring and her heart was heavy with foreboding. Her pain was eased only by the recollection of Father Pierron ministering to enemy warriors who had been wounded during the attack. She knew he would be there to comfort the doomed prisoners, speaking softly and praying. He would explain that *Rawanniio* would be waiting for them when death took them, that they would have life everlasting once they were baptized.

Mohawks always prolonged the agony of their enemies. For three days the drums beat without ceasing. Guns were fired, the villagers sang and feasted. On the third day the Mohicans, thirteen men and four women, were cruelly tortured and put to death. The brave warriors gave no sound while their captives cut the flesh from the dying bodies of the most courageous. It was believed that their courage could be transferred to the drinkers of blood. But only when death was imminent did the doomed men sing their death songs. A few of the prisoners screamed during their agonies, but it was permissible. These were *women*.

The celebrations of torture excited the villagers and the taste for whiskey was strong. Casks of rum and brandy were brought from Fort Orange. Tekakwitha huddled inside the long house of Iowerano, praying the grotesque celebrations would end.

Father Pierron begged the Turtle Clan to stop the tortures, but the Mohawks laughed. He tended the suffering and begged for permission to baptize. The Mohawks grumbled: "Why should the *rakeni* treat our enemies so well? Is he, too, the enemy?"

Standing in the burning field with its smell of charred flesh in the air, Father Pierron appealed to the people. In the language of the Iroquois he told of the Sermon on the Mount. "You must love your enemies," he cried. "You must prepare your souls for one day, you, too, will meet *Rawanniio* face to face. Allow me to baptize the dying so that they may go to heaven."

"Baptize the devils," Iowerano yelled. "You waste your time. There will be no heaven for Mohicans!"

The sacrifices to *Areskoui* were finally effused and families went back to their long houses, exhausted from the three day orgy. Work had been neglected during the period of restitution. Now the town of Caughnawaga returned to the task of living. It was a relief to Tekakwitha. She resumed her chores as she usually did, cheerfully and willingly.

Once again, Iowerano's family completed their annual fishing trip to the Cascades and almost as soon as they returned Kryn paid a visit to Iowerano.

As she ground corn for the evening meal, Tekakwitha heard the ensuing conversation. She had always admired Kryn and as she glanced at the tall warrior she saw that today he wore a wolf's head cap and a string of giant bears' claws around his neck. Tekakwitha knew the good, soft-spoken wife of this man and spoke to her often at the spring or in the fields.

Iowerano, his thin lips disappearing in a tight line, beckoned Kryn to be seated. The guest lowered himself to the floor and sat cross-legged on a reed mat that had been spread for him. His smooth, dark face, serious and proud, softened in a smile. "You have asked me to come," he said.

Iowerano nodded, the coxcomb on his head moving back and forth. "Yes, Kryn. I have words to say. Your friendship with the French devils offends me."

Kryn continued to smile. "Iowerano knows how weakened we have become. There have been too many wars. Why does he resist the French who have grown so powerful?"

"You have forgotten, Kryn, but my memory is long. From the very beginning, the French spilled our blood. From the days of Champlain, French muskets have taken the life's breath from our people."

Kryn waited patiently. "It was not the blackrobes who did the killing," he said.

"Too willingly have you accepted the blackrobes' belief." Iowerano's eyes disappeared in narrow slits. "And you have forsaken *Areskoui*." Iowerano turned away in disgust.

"Yes. I have done so. I do not pretend to do otherwise. It makes no sense to me to make sacrifices to a god who spills blood. The League is slowly abandoning *Areskoui*. And the rum, the whiskey, is destroying our people. Even you cannot deny that. We should leave the Dutch to their liquor and trade our furs to the French."

Iowerano's eyes swelled; he inhaled deeply and seemed speechless for a moment. "Does Kryn know what he is proposing?"

"Yes, Iowerano. I know full well. The League has made peace with the powerful French. They have agreed to accept the blackrobes and still some of our people

burn the chapels of these men and destroy their posses-
sions. That is not acceptable."

Iowerano stared into the fire. For a long time he said
nothing. Then he turned to Kryn and said. "I have great
difficulty accepting blackrobes."

Kryn shrugged. "We are moving into a new time,
Iowerano. I am a loyal and true Mohawk, but I see that
we must change."

Long after Kryn departed, Iowerano sat in gloomy
silence. Tekakwitha timidly offered water, but her uncle
merely shook his head. Quietly she walked from the long
house into the bright sun of the day. Draping her blanket
over her head she hurried to the cornfields. Enita was
already there. The lapping of the water against the shore
of the Mohawk River and the rustle of dried corn leaves
moving in the wind soothed the soul of Tekakwitha.
Areskoui, the drinker of blood, the killer of enemies, was
dying. Kryn had said so. *Rawanniio* was here beneath the
blue sky, here in her heart. She picked up her hoe and
went to work.

Chapter Seven

Karitha draped strands of heavy wampum beads around the neck of Tekakwitha, braceleted her arms and wrists, adorned her hair with ribbons and beads. Even her tunic, leggings and moccasins were heavily encrusted with beads. She had celebrated her seventeenth birthday.

"It is time," Karitha said. "Certainly you are old enough to marry. You must attend the dances, mingle with the young braves. Why do you stay to yourself so much of the time?"

"I am happiest that way," Tekakwitha replied, a hint of sadness in her dark eyes.

"There will be a dance in the great circle tomorrow. You must go."

Tekakwitha went to the dance to please her aunts. It was her nature to please; it was difficult for her to defy. But she remained shyly on the sidelines, pulling her blanket over her head and shoulders. Karitha and Arosen glowered in the shadows, sharing unpleasant, whispered words.

"Go to her," Arosen said. "You are her mother. She must obey you."

"Tekakwitha," Karitha said sternly, "remove your blanket to show off your ornaments. You will attract the best young braves that way. You, a chief's daughter."

Tekakwitha looked down at her moccasins. "Please Aunt, I don't wish to take part in the dancing."

Karitha pursed her lips, turned to Arosen and whispered. "She should be grateful for whomever she gets. Foolish Algonquin that she is."

Tekakwitha brought her hands to her rough cheeks. She would never have the smooth glowing cheeks of a young Mohawk maiden. But Iowerano repeatedly said, "Tekakwitha is cheerful and industrious. The best of the young braves will be happy to gain the hand of a chief's daughter such as Tekakwitha. Everyone loves her." Iowerano's words brought comfort, but Tekakwitha's heart had renounced marriage long ago.

Behind Iowerano's back, Karitha smirked. "He is old. He has forgotten what attracts the young brave." And Arosen nodded. "Men change when the years weigh heavily upon their backs."

In her gentle way Tekakwitha continued to resist the entreaties of her aunts.

As time went on Karitha and Arosen pressured Tekakwitha more and more to take part in activities that involved the braves. Tekakwitha refused, not in the vein of disobedience, but more in a manner of pleading. "I am not ready," she said. "Please, I am not ready. I will go to the *gan-a-shote* dance and I will dance alone. I am not ready to dance with the braves."

Arosen and Karitha exchanged sour looks.

"You are not a true Mohawk," scolded Karitha. "You are like your Algonquin mother, weak and disloyal. Your refusal to marry brings shame to the house of Iowerano."

Tekakwitha turned away, a hurt expression clouding her face. They don't understand, she thought. I am like my mother, but I am my father's daughter as well. I am a true and loyal Mohawk.

Arosen applied Karitha's tactics, but in addition to the scoldings and railings, she demanded that Tekakwitha perform difficult tasks and then complained that they were done poorly.

Tekakwitha tried harder to please her aunts, but the more she tried the more belligerent they became. Slowly now her determination not to marry was growing stronger. Alone in the forest, the wind whispering through the leaves, she spoke to the true God. "Why am I so different? Why am I not like the others? It has always been so. The girls wear their finest adornments and take joy in this. I am happiest when no one takes notice of me. This angers Karitha and Arosen, but no matter what happens, I cannot marry. Please help me *Rawanniio*. I want things to remain as they are."

Once again autumn crept into the Mohawk valley, bringing the season of color and harvest. One day when Tekakwitha worked in the cornfields close to the shore, a canoe came swiftly down the river and stopped near the gardens. It carried a blackrobe.

Father Boniface stepped from the canoe, clutching a small box. He brought nothing else. Some of the villagers followed behind the priest; a few walked alongside him. There had always been curiosity when a stranger came to the village and a new blackrobe was no exception.

Iowerano, true to his steadfast intolerance, turned his back to the priest, again instructing his family to have nothing to do with the newcomer who came to assist Father Pierron.

Before long the two priests built a larger chapel with their own labor. It was a long house that they furnished with pictures they painted themselves, a crucifix, a crude altar on which to celebrate Mass, and rush mats for the floor.

Inwardly, Tekakwitha was excited about the new chapel. She heard some of the women describe the beauty of it and she treasured every word, but out of obedience to Iowerano she kept silent. Her longing to join the Christians was becoming almost unbearable. Her blood raced with desire to learn about and know the true God. She dreamed of kneeling inside the chapel and worshipping with the Christians.

Karitha and Arosen had not given up the idea of finding a husband for Tekakwitha and they were determined that one way or another they would marry her off. They no longer spoke to her about the matter, pretending to have lost interest. She believed her aunts had abandoned the idea and when Karitha and Arosen whispered their secret conversations and laughed together, Tekakwitha was pleased at their good humor.

One evening Karitha commanded Tekakwitha to dress appropriately for company. "Put on your finest wampum beads, earrings, bracelets and ribbons. You must look like the daughter of a chief."

Karitha brought out her face paint. "I will oil and comb your hair, Tekakwitha. You must look pretty. And I think it best you wear a little paint on your cheeks and lips. Here, let me paint you."

Tekakwitha turned away. She wanted no part of face paint or finery, but Karitha persisted.

The long house had been swept clean. The pots, wampum belts, furs and other skins hung on pegs against the walls. The benches were adorned with rich beaver pelts and a long reed mat was spread before the hearth. The household of Iowerano awaited its honored guests.

The visitors arrived and it was Tekakwitha who greeted them. She recognized Okwire, a handsome brave whom she saw at the last dance. His parents followed and if Tekakwitha had not been so shy, if she had not looked away so quickly, she would have noticed that Okwire carried a bundle of shiny furs, gifts for the family of Iowerano.

Iowerano began the conversation. "Welcome to our hearth. We are honored to share our evening meal with you."

Karitha offered nuts and berries, Arosen served a tea sweetened with maple syrup. With a nod of her head, Karitha directed Tekakwitha to serve the *sagamite*.

Okwire's mother smiled pleasantly, the flames from the fire falling softly on her face. Okwire's father, dressed in painted skins, strings of beads, and feathers tied to a long braid that hung down his back, appeared to be content and happy. The evening was warm, peaceful and pleasant. A little breeze, born on the river had found its way into the long house through the open doorway.

Tekakwitha held a steaming bowl of *sagamite*, cupped with a reed protector. As she was about to serve Okwire she suddenly pulled the bowl away as if she had been burned. At once everything became clear to her. The moment she would transfer the *sagamite* to Okwire's bowl she would be engaged to him in marriage! That was the Mohawk way.

Tekakwitha's smile faded. She said not a word, but carefully set the bowl of *sagamite* next to Karitha and rushed from the long house.

Her small feet moved swiftly down the slope to the water's edge. She settled on the sand in the shade of the corn stalks. Tears welled up in her eyes, rolled down her rough painted cheeks and fell upon her purple wampum. It wasn't anger that filled her heart. It was sadness,

sadness that her aunts would try to trick her into a marriage she disdained.

Footsteps padded the sand and when Tekakwitha looked up she stared into the angry eyes of her aunt. "Come back, Tekakwitha, foolish girl. It is not too late to repair what you have done. Do not disgrace the house of Iowerano. Come back and all will still be right."

Unwaveringly, Tekakwitha's eyes met the black angry eyes of her aunt. "I am not coming back. I am not marrying Okwire or anyone. I would rather die."

Fury clouded Karitha's face. She turned and bounded up the hill to the long house.

Okwire and his family had left hurriedly. Tekakwitha was sorry at having caused her uncle embarrassment, but she couldn't help herself. She knew what she wanted and she didn't want to marry.

Slowly she went back to the house on heavy feet. Iowerano said nothing, but stared at her with a fierceness she understood. She had made him unhappy and angry. Karitha and Arosen became sullen and the mood continued until it was time for bed. Long after the family fell asleep, Tekakwitha lay on her sleeping shelf, sleepless and guilt-ridden for having offended Iowerano and her aunts. She felt stronger, however, for having openly defended her position. She could not have done otherwise. She prayed to *Rawanniio* that he might make her family understand.

The next morning was no better. Karitha and Arosen spoke to her only when they needed to. She was relieved when the morning sun rose higher in the sky. It was the beginning of the corn festival and she would meet with the other girls and take part in the corn husking. This had always been a joyful time, a time she looked forward to every year. The young girls of Caughnawaga gathered every autumn to celebrate the harvest. Enita was already there in the clearing, the husking had begun.

A small mountain of ripe maize and white flint had been gathered here. This was one of the happiest of Mohawk celebrations, carried on in a festive spirit, with songs, laughter and joking. It was the oldest tradition, enjoyed by everyone.

The older women sat on the edges of the clearing and watched the happy girls. The men retired nearby, smoked their pipes and told stories of glorious days past. The young braves watched the girls, too, and the maidens always wore their finest dresses and wampum, conscious of the attention. A few of the girls wore cotton dresses that came from Fort Orange, but Tekakwitha preferred the deer skin tunic.

Tekakwitha sat down on the sand next to Enita.

"You're late," Enita said, making room for her sister. Already Enita had several bundles of corn beside her, twenty ears braided together in each bunch. Tekakwitha lifted a heavy ear of corn and tore a section of leaves from the cob. Her face suddenly glowed with color. The kernels were straight and plump, and...red!

Tonedetta had been watching Tekakwitha since the moment she came and she called out teasingly, "Okwire! Okwire! It is a sign! It is a sign!"

"You know, Tekakwitha," Enita whispered, "the first red ear is a sign that you have an admirer close by."

Tekakwitha couldn't help but smile at Tonedetta's jesting. It was all good fun. It had always been one of the most delightful moments of the harvest festival. But just as Tekakwitha was about to put her red ear down and pick up another, she glanced up and saw that Tonedetta had unsheathed a crooked ear of corn, tapered and bent like a little old man. Tekakwitha pointed and cried out in a loud voice, "Wagemin. Wagemin. Paimosaid!"

Whenever a girl unsheathed a crooked ear of corn, she suffered the laughter and humor of all the others. It meant that she had an old ugly admirer nearby. At once the girls began to sing the song of the Algonquin, "The little old corn thief, walker at night. The little old cornthief, walker at night." Tonedetta's admirer was a little old man, not a handsome young brave!

Ripples of laughter rose on the crisp evening air. Tonedetta covered her face with her hands, but her shoulders shook with laughter. Even the old men laughed, enjoying the rollicking good time. The harvesters sang:

"*Wagemin. Wagemin.*
Thief in the blade,
Blight of the cornfield
Paimosaid."

Enita laughed. "You are a good sport, Tekakwitha. Tonedetta is, too. The song is Algonquin but the Mohawks sing it, also. See," she said pointing, "even Karitha and Arosen are laughing."

Tekakwitha glanced at her aunts. It was true, they were laughing. Perhaps they had forgiven her.

Chapter Eight

Tekakwitha continued to pray in the private of the forest or in the quiet of her heart when she worked inside the long house or in the fields. Her aunts remained sullen, but she accepted their treatment cheerfully.

The priests at Caughnawaga did not pressure the Indians to accept the Catholic faith. Instruction in the teachings was most important. The priests had to be certain that the intentions of the Indians were serious and true.

Autumn had come quickly to Caughnawaga in 1670. The maples, oaks and birch trees turned red, yellow and brilliant orange. The leaves fell one by one; traces of frost lay hidden in shallow spots. In the morning bark buckets mirrored thin sheets of ice on the water's surface and Tekakwitha knew winter was lurking nearby. Still there were "Indian Summer" days when warm sunshine briefly brought summer back. It was such a day when Tekakwitha paused at the spring with her water jars, her red blanket draped about her head and shoulders. Enita had come so quietly Tekakwitha was unaware of her presence until her stepsister spoke.

"Tekakwitha," she said softly, almost in a whisper. "I tell you this and no one else. Iowerano will hate me when he finds out."

Tekakwitha's expression revealed concern. "What have you done? Is it something I can help you with?"

"No one can help me. When Iowerano finds out he will have nothing more to do with me. I have married Onas, the Christian. Now I, too, will take the 'prayer.'"

The news took Tekakwitha's breath away. For a few moments she didn't speak. Then she threw her arms around Enita and said, "I wish you well, Enita. You will be happy now."

"I will miss you little sister," Enita said, her eyes glistening.

Tekakwitha longed to tell her stepsister of her yearning to become a Christian, but she held back. She kept the secret locked in her heart. "Iowerano will be angry," she said, "but *Rawanniio* will bless you."

Tekakwitha walked slowly back to the long house, feeling the loss of something dear, yet joy for her stepsister overshadowed her feelings.

When she entered the long house she came upon a volatile scene. The fierce look in Iowerano's eyes told her that he had learned of Enita's marriage to Onas. His words were sharp and thunderous. "Never will any of you mention the name of Enita in this house. She is dead to us now."

Karitha's voice cracked with fury. "Ungrateful girl! After all we have done for her."

The veins on Iowerano's temples stood out in the stressful fury of hate. He picked up his musket and bounded out the door to comfort himself in the sport of hunting.

Arosen turned to Tekakwitha. "May you be a better daughter than that snipe of a girl, Enita. It is the fault of the hated blackrobes. The blackrobes have brought nothing but trouble."

Iowerano, Karitha and Arosen still harbored seeds of hatred and distrust of the blackrobes. Tekakwitha observed all of this and worried that her family would eventually suspect that she, too, yearned to become a Christian. But Tekakwitha's yearning was slowly becoming an obsession.

More often now she fled to the forest and knelt beneath the tall pine. She had seen the Christians on their knees and she knew this was the way to pray. "You are here, *Rawanniio*. I know you are with me every minute. I want to please you. I love you. Help me to love you more. Help me to become a Christian."

Tekakwitha saw that Christians were treated with contempt in the Castle of the Turtles. The blackrobes forbade drinking and this was a habit the Mohawks found difficult to break. Fighting had been a way of life. Evil had been excused, *Areskuoi*, the evil *Manitou*, had been blamed. The Mohawks still clung to many of the old ways.

The peaceful teachings of Christianity were more easily accepted by the children. Yet when any kind of disaster struck, the Christians were blamed. The villagers screamed insults and threw stones. Many of the older Christians worshipped in private.

When the Castle of the Turtles was still refusing to accept the blackrobes, the Onendagachief, Ganeagowa, traveled to Quebec. Father Fremin had his mission at La Prairie across the river from Montreal and Chief Ganeagowa spent a happy time at this Christian colony. One day he returned to Caughnawaga with startling news.

There was a hint of snow in the air, the trees were bare. Everyone gathered in the village circle, wrapping their blankets tightly about them. Chief Ganeagowa was a great chief and his words were always received with attention.

"I have come back to tell you that I have accepted the Christian faith," he said, his arms folded, his jaw firmly set. The crowd became hushed and silent, almost speechless.

"I have been baptized and my name is Joseph Ganeagowa. Satekon, as you know has embraced the Catholic faith, good wife that she is, and we will move to La Prairie, the settlement of Christians. If any of you wish to accompany me and Satekon, I welcome you."

Ganeagowa's shocking words brought silence, then an outcry. Above the noise of the angry crowd, Iowerano shouted, "Never will I call you by a Christian name. I will not call you Joseph. I will not even call you Ganeagowa. I will call you TRAITOR! You turn your back on your own and embrace the hated blackrobes. Your decision can only weaken our nation more."

Ganeagowa stood straighter, taller. "I am not a traitor. I love our tribe, our people. I have seen what evil the Dutch whiskey brings to our villages. I have seen the immoral actions of our young and our old. I have seen the difference between our people and the Christians. The Christians have found happiness in the one true God." Chief Ganeagowa raised his hand. "Please don't hate us. We want to live among you in peace."

Iowerano scowled. He had no answer for Joseph Ganeagowa. He had no answer for the Christians. He spat, turned his back and left the meeting.

Immediately, Joseph Ganeagowa prepared to leave for La Prarie. Enita and Onas, Anastasia, and twenty-five other Mohawks spent the remainder of the week getting their canoes ready and packing their belongings.

The morning of the departure for La Prarie came and the Christians met on the shore. Tekakwitha wrapped her blanket tightly and turned to leave the long house. She had to see Enita one last time. Karitha and Arosen prepared to go, not because of Enita, but because they were curious to see the party off.

As soon as Tekakwitha and her aunts were about to leave, Iowerano loomed in the doorway, his eyes bulging, his nostrils flaring. He stretched his arm across the doorway and said, "I forbid all of you. No one from the house of Iowerano will give approval to the Christians. Ganeagowa has gone crazy. No one in my family will be on the shore to wish him well. Get back to work!"

Tekakwitha trembled behind her partitioned space. She picked up her sewing and put pressure on the needle, but her fingers shook and she dropped the work to her lap. Iowerano had looked directly into her eyes and in so doing he seemed to look into her soul. Could he have guessed her burning desire to become a Christian? Could he know how much she longed to worship the one true God, the God he hated?

In the days that followed, Tekakwitha in her shy, gentle manner went about her daily tasks. She prepared food for the family and served it. She visited the sick and brought food to the elderly. The whole village loved her. She worked hard in the fields, planting, weeding and tending the crops. She sewed in her spare time, creating beautiful garments decorated with porcupine quills she dyed herself. Her beadwork was intricate and fine. Iowerano was justly proud. All the while she remained obedient and cheerful and many times during the course of each day she said silent prayers to *Rawanniio*. But her heart was breaking. She was not one step closer to becoming a Christian. Yet she was developing a stronger conviction. Each morning when she greeted the splendor of a new day and each evening when the sun sank behind the trees, she asked God to help her find a way and she was sure that he would.

Chapter Nine

Summer with its quiet beauty came once again to the Mohawk valley. Tekakwitha was now eighteen. Karitha and Arosen grumbled and complained, but Tekakwitha remained unmarried.

Father Boniface left Caughnawaga. His health had deteriorated beneath the yoke of hard work and austere conditions. Tekakwitha wept to see him leave. She took comfort in his presence in the village. On many occasions she had made up her mind to speak to him, but at the last moment courage failed her. The fear of Iowerano and loyalty to him still held her back.

A new missionary, Father James de Lamberville, arrived at Caughnawaga. He was eager to serve the Mohawks who by now had grudgingly accepted the blackrobes though they disdained the Catholic faith. Iowerano continued to defy the decree of the League. He refused to welcome any blackrobe that came to the village.

One morning Karitha rushed into the lodge breathless and excited.

"You will never guess, not in many moons, Arosen.

Kryn has left his Christian wife! They have had a grave misunderstanding and he has deserted her and the child."

Arosen's eyes grew wide, her round face shone with an expression of mischief. "They have kept to themselves, living on the edge of the settlement, but I've heard that things were not going well."

Karitha smiled slyly, her eyes narrowing. "Kryn is a handsome one. Perhaps he went to another village to take a new wife. I wouldn't be surprised."

Arosen nodded. "It serves his wife right, she and her Christian ways. All Christians are troublemakers."

Tekakwitha turned to her sewing, saddened to hear what Kryn had done. She had always looked up to Kryn. It made her especially sad to hear that the Christians were blamed whenever anything went wrong. Most people believed that when any evil befell the village, the Christians were the cause of it.

Though her eyesight had improved slightly, Tekakwitha continued to have difficulty seeing, especially in bright sunlight. Always there were chores that were waiting to be done. Desiring to be away from the long house, away from the biting tongues of her aunts, she went out to gather wood for the hearth. She hurried on her way and failed to see the gnarled roots of an old tree that crossed her path. Before she could sustain her balance, her moccasin got caught in a tangle of wood and she twisted her ankle. For a few minutes the pain paralyzed her. She rubbed her ankle and hobbled back to the long house. By the time she got inside her ankle had swelled and Karitha was forced to cut the legging.

"Stay in and rest," Karitha said. "No use to stand and work. It will only make it worse. I have bound the sprain and if you stay off your feet it will heal. You must be well by harvest time. We will need you to help."

Tekakwitha hung her head. If only she had been more careful. If only she had seen the mass of roots that lay on the path. Her aunts were pleased when she was able to work. She pleased them more when she took over many of their own duties.

"I will sew, Aunt," she said quickly. "I will finish the eel skin bands you wanted. I'm sorry I cannot help you in the gardens. I promise to work harder once I am well."

Karitha and Arosen left for the fields, Arosen grumbling as she hurried to keep up with her sister. It had not rained in several weeks and the corn would die unless it were hand watered. Iowerano, jubilant from a streak of exceptional hunting, hurried out into the forest. Tekakwitha was alone in the dim silence of the long house.

On this day, Father de Lamberville was making the rounds in the village, introducing himself. When he came to the house of Iowerano he paused at the open door. Tekakwitha heard his footsteps, saw his shadow in the doorway. It fell across the floor where sunlight had made a small bright path. The silver cross that hung from the priest's wide girdle flashed against the dark walls and Tekakwitha held her breath. She knew the shadow belonged to Father de Lamberville.

The pause was momentary. Slowly, almost reluctantly, the shadow began to retreat. Tekakwitha put down her sewing with trembling fingers. She wanted to call out, but there in the quiet shadows she was unable to move. If she let this opportunity pass, when would she ever have a chance to speak to the blackrobe? Perhaps never. She rose to her feet, smothering a cry of pain when she put her weight on her sore foot, and hobbled to the doorway.

She opened her mouth to speak and for a moment

she seemed to have no voice. Then breathless and with forced effort she called out timidly, "It is I, Tekakwitha."

Father de Lamberville turned back and smiled. He was surprised to be greeted by a member of Iowerano's household. He was well aware of the chief's views, and believed that never would a blackrobe be admitted to the house of this Mohawk. But now Tekakwitha was standing outside in the bright sunshine, calling to him.

Tekakwitha's breath came faster. Did she have the courage to tell the *rakeni* of her desire to become a Christian? Certainly she was old enough to decide for herself. But how should she begin? Would the priest think her strange? She took a deep breath and in a clear determined voice she couldn't believe was her own, she said, "*Rakeni?*"

"Yes, Tekakwitha. Did you wish to speak with me?"

Tekakwitha stood in the doorway, the sun forcing her to bring her hand to her brow. She squinted at the priest and supported herself by grasping the bark frame of the house with one hand.

The blackrobe's expression changed. "Do you need help?" he asked. "I will call one of the women to help you."

Tekakwitha smiled, her courage blossoming. "I am not hurting. Only my soul. I...I want with all of my heart to become...to become...a Christian!"

Father de Lamberville's eye brows came together. "But, your uncle, Iowerano. They tell me he even forbids the mention of the blackrobes in his house."

"Yes, that is true. But I am old enough now to decide for myself. I want to know the one true God, *Rawanniio*. I want...I want to be baptized!"

The priest frowned. "Would you defy your father to become a Christian?"

Tekakwitha nodded. "Even if my father should

punish me or banish me, I want to be a child of *Rawanniio*. I would die for that. Please help me."

Father de Lamberville spent a few moments in thought and studied Tekakwitha's face before he answered. "Yes, child, I will help you. As soon as you are able, you may receive instructions. I will teach you the 'prayer,' and I will baptize you."

Tears streamed down Tekakwitha's face, but she was smiling. She could not remember having been happier.

That night when Iowerano and his family gathered for the evening meal, Tekakwitha was more silent than usual. Her decision was firm. Nothing could make her change her mind, though she was at a loss as to how to make her conviction known to her family. What kind of punishment would Iowerano give her? Would he banish her? Perhaps he wouldn't be able to control his anger. He might kill her.

Karitha glanced sideways at Tekakwitha and smirked. "You aren't yourself, Tekakwitha. What are you up to?"

Tekakwitha wanted to speak out, divulge her decision to become a Christian. But was this the right time? Perhaps she should wait until her ankle healed.

Iowerano looked extremely glum. When things went badly at hunting, he came home to sulk. This evening he stared into the fire in gloomy silence. Fearing her stepfather's foul mood, Tekakwitha remained silent.

Hearing his wife's question, Iowerano turned his attention to his daughter. Arosen, too, scrutinized Tekakwitha's face, who blushed now and gazed at her dinner. "I am just in a very happy mood," she said.

The family looked from one to the other. Arosen smiled suspiciously.

"Perhaps," she said, "Tekakwitha has found someone

to marry. And we have been worrying about her all this while."

Tekakwitha's cheeks burned and she brought her fingers to her lips to suppress a cry. She did not regret her decision to become a Christian. She regretted only that her family would hate her when they found out.

During the following days, Tekakwitha prayed to *Rawanniio* for strength and courage so that she could tell Iowerano of her decision. She knew he would be angry and she was prepared for anything, anything as long as she could become a child of the one true God.

The days wore on and she became stronger in her conviction, more determined that her decision was correct. Her ankle had healed and the time had come to tell Iowerano.

Storm clouds moved in, the sky grew dark. The rain finally came, hard at first, then quietly fell upon the roof of the long house. It drenched the corn fields, keeping the women inside. Iowerano sat cross-legged on his mat, dozing off now and then, dreaming perhaps of days past. Tekakwitha sat down beside him.

"Uncle."

Iowerano's heavy lidded eyes fluttered, then opened.

Something came alive in Tekakwitha. An inner strength that had lain smoldering for so many years suddenly burst into flames. She looked unflinchingly into her uncle's eyes.

"I have never disobeyed you, Uncle."

Startled, Iowerano stared at his stepdaughter.

"That is true." He was fully roused now and he brought his drooping shoulders back. "What have you done now?" he asked, his voice rising. "I have never seen you in this manner."

Tekakwitha's gaze didn't waver. Her small body

trembled, but her voice was resolute and determined, no longer timid. "I know how strongly you feel about Christians, but I cannot help myself. I have asked the blackrobe for baptism. I...I want to become a Christian."

Hearing the words of his adopted daughter brought a look of violence to Iowerano's face. His eyes bulged from their bony sockets, his large nostrils flared and for a time he was speechless. His face, like brown polished leather, shone by the light of the fire and he cried out in a loud voice, "Ha! Enita! And now *you*!"

Tekakwitha's eyes held his gaze. She stared at her uncle with the conviction of a true Mohawk. "I am sorry. That is what I must do and do it I will!"

All the fury and anger Iowerano had for Christians, all the hatred he had harbored so tenaciously all the past years exploded into a violent rage. He raised his hand as if to strike Tekakwitha and she waited for the blow to fall. Instead, he threw his pipe to the floor, muttered under his breath and hurried out into the night.

Karitha and Arosen had been listening nearby. Tekakwitha had not even been aware of their presence, so intent was she upon speaking to Iowerano. But now the two women unleashed their wrath, not only upon Tekakwitha, but on all the Christians. "You are worse than dead, Tekakwitha," Arosen yelled. "You are a disgrace to the house of your uncle. Hateful girl!"

Karitha feigned tears. "All these years I worked to bring you up right and you reward me like this. You will see. No good will come of this. You will be punished and well you deserve it."

"I can only hope so," said Arosen. "Iowerano has always had a special affection for this...this stupid Algonquin. I could never understand why."

Tekakwitha bowed her head. "I mean no harm to anyone," she said gently. "And yes, I am Algonquin, but

I am a Mohawk, too. I want to become a Christian and live in peace."

But peace was not something Tekakwitha enjoyed. Karitha and Arosen burdened Tekakwitha with chores, meting out more work than she was physically capable of doing. They scolded, ridiculed and abused her. The commonplace atmosphere of the long house of Iowerano came to an end.

Chapter Ten

Several weeks passed, but Iowerano rarely spoke to his stepdaughter. Most of the time he ignored her. Tekakwitha was saddened by his ill treatment. If only he would speak to me, she thought. I would welcome harsh words, even punishment, but the silence? It is as if he does not see me. As if I am not here, as if I am dead.

Karitha and Arosen continued their planned torment. Tekakwitha accepted every antagonism without complaining. Every day she went to the praying house where Father de Lamberville gave her instructions in the Catholic faith. She learned about the life of Christ and the knowledge brought joy to her heart. However, the time away from the long house had to be repaid and she was forced to awaken earlier every morning to begin her work before sunlight.

One evening a child peeked inside the long house and shouted, "Kryn is back! Kryn is back!" Everyone including Tekakwitha rushed outside to see Kryn.

"Why has Kryn come back?" Karitha asked Arosen.

Arosen shrugged. "He must have heard that his child died. But it is too late. She has been long buried."

Kryn strode through the village as handsome as ever. It was soon learned that he had not come back to stay. He had come back to get his Christian wife. He, too, had been baptized a Christian and now wanted to be off to the praying castle to live.

"They have all lost their minds," Iowerano growled, indignant and angry. Karitha and Arosen stayed out of his way. Only Tekakwitha waited on him and brought him his meals. He looked past her, away from her, ignoring her presence. His last trade at Fort Orange had enriched him with a cask of rum. He had announced that it would be used only as medicine during the cold weather, but he opened it now and drowned his sorrows in a gourd cup of whiskey.

Kryn soon left Caughnawaga, taking with him his wife and a few Christians.

The Christians who remained at the Castle of the Turtles began to prepare for Christmas. Tekakwitha was filled with excitement. Father de Lamberville was planning special services and the children were rehearsing hymns that were sung in Iroquois. Their sweet voices could be heard at practice every day. Tekakwitha went twice a day to the chapel, once for instructions and again in the evening to pray.

Tekakwitha could hardly wait until Christmas day. Christians whispered when they were at work, telling of the wonderful display Father de Lamberville had brought from Quebec. It had come on a great ship all the way from France. The church had been decorated with garlands of pine boughs and red berries, the benches covered with shiny beaver pelts. A pine tree had been brought into the chapel, heavy with strings of popcorn, berries and nuts. But all of these things were nothing compared to the sight that met their eyes Christmas morning.

On one side of the altar where the decorated pine tree stood, a small crib nestled in boughs of pine. There in the crib lay a beautiful statue of the Christ Child. The pink porcelain cherub was something none of the Indians had ever seen before. They looked upon it with amazement and awe and so did Tekakwitha. She loved the story of the Christ Child's birth and she was filled with happiness whenever it was told. But going home to the house of Iowerano was anything but peaceful. The aunts scolded and Iowerano pouted. Tekakwitha walked on tiptoes, silently coming and going on feet as light as the down of milkweed.

Father de Lamberville was more than satisfied with Tekakwitha's progress. "You are a model Christian, Tekakwitha. You are a rare pupil. You lived as a Christian from your earliest childhood."

"Please, Father," Tekakwitha said, "please baptize me. I want to attend Mass and worship *Rawanniio*."

Father de Lamberville pondered her words and then said, "Tekakwitha, there is no point in prolonging baptism. I will baptize you on Easter Sunday."

Tekakwitha bowed her head in deep humility; tears of joy wet her cheeks. What she had hoped for so long would finally come true. Now if only Iowerano and her aunts would accept her conversion things would be so wonderful.

Gradually, Iowerano forgot his malice toward Tekakwitha. Grudgingly he spoke to her, but only when it became necessary.

"Iowerano has not forgiven you," Karitha warned. "He will never recognize your conversion. You have won him over with your smiles and your kind ways, but I see through you."

Arosen shook a finger in Tekakwitha's face. "You don't fool me either. Your Christian ways will get you into more trouble. You will see."

Tekakwitha looked forward to Easter Sunday with triumphant joy that overshadowed the unhappiness at home. Each day her soul grew closer to *Rawanniio*. She continued to worship in the forest where the pure whiteness of new fallen snow erased her tracks that led to the tree where she had carved the cross.

"I am not worthy, *Rawanniio*," she said over and over. "I am not worthy, but I want to be your child, close to you forever. Please help me to love you more. If Iowerano and my aunts continue to despise the path I have taken, then I am willing to accept whatever comes. Your will be done."

Karitha and Arosen's wrath brought pain, but for every mean and spiteful word, Tekakwitha replied with a smile and a cheerful answer. Sundays were dedicated to God and Christians refrained from work. Tekakwitha refused to work, too. This incensed her aunts even more.

The winter spent itself in one last meager snowfall and Easter Sunday morning dawned bright and beautiful. The sun caressed the tall pines, the budding oaks and the maples. Tekakwitha and two other girls dressed in deer skin tunics and leggings, with white blankets covering their heads, solemnly stood at the baptismal fount to receive the sacrament of baptism. Tekakwitha wore no wampum, no jewelry or finery. She had given that up, realizing that prayers were more pleasing to God.

The chapel was decorated with garlands of flowers and vines. The open windows let in a warm spring breeze that came off the river. Along with the gentle wind came the sound of birds singing. Tekakwitha was overjoyed. She stood, her hands folded while Father de Lamberville poured the holy water upon her head and said, "I baptize thee, Kateri Tekakwitha, in the name of the Father, Son, and Holy Ghost. Amen."

Tears rolled down Tekakwitha's cheeks. She was at peace, ecstatic and happy. Her heart seemed near to bursting. This was the day she had dreamed of. This was the day she had longed for. Now she was a Christian! She was a child of the one true God! The Christian name she had chosen was Catherine and the Mohawk version was Kateri.

Each day she went to the chapel early in the morning for Mass and then again in the evening to pray. She did more than her share of work. Karitha found more and more tasks for her to do. Tekakwitha struggled to do all that was expected of her. One thing she refused to do, however, was work on Sunday. This was the Lord's day.

"You are lazy, Tekakwitha," Arosen railed. "You want to get out of work and so you use your new religion as an excuse. And we will never call you Kateri."

"You are too easy on Tekakwitha," Arosen scolded. "Those who do not work should not eat!"

Karitha smiled. "You are right, Arosen. If Tekakwitha refuses to work on Sunday, she shall not eat on that day. We will hide the food. If she gets hungry enough she will change her ways."

Tekakwitha walked to the chapel, her head down, her blanket pulled low over her forehead. She felt the first blow with surprise. When she turned, she saw a group of children. They were laughing and jeering and then she caught the second blow on her back. The children were throwing stones at her and cursing. She touched her face and felt a trickle of warm blood ooze from her cheek.

How could these small innocents behave so? They were just children. Then she heard a boy call out, "Iowerano wants her punished. Don't stop! She is worse than a dog!"

So, Iowerano had planned this for her, hoping to discourage her from her conviction and new found faith. Did he think her belief was so weak she would give it up because of a little pain? But fear swept over her. Perhaps this was only the beginning.

Chapter Eleven

Mass was ended and Kateri Tekakwitha lingered at the altar. "*Rawanniio*," she whispered, "you are the reason for my being. Help me to be pleasing in your sight. Everything that I do is for your glory. I love you with my whole soul, my whole heart and my whole mind. Help me to have a perfect love for you, my one true God."

Today was Sunday and not a day of work. Kateri would, however, bring water to the long house. The rest of the day would be spent sewing and praying.

The breeze was balmy, the sky was bright blue above the tall pines. The grass had grown taller; it was harder to see the wild flowers. She had to bend low to see them. When she stood, the whole world turned dark. She felt faint and light-headed. Struggling to maintain her balance she held on to the trunk of a small maple. She had experienced the same dizziness before. Perhaps it was from fasting the previous week or it may have been brought on by the strenuous tasks her aunts imposed. A few times Arosen insisted that Kateri work in the fields on Sunday and because this was a Christian holy day it broke her heart to obey her aunts. On days she didn't work, Karitha and Arosen refused to allow her to eat. She often ate berries or nuts she gathered; that was all.

She took a deep breath and sat down to fight off the weakness. Suddenly, and it seemed as if from nowhere, a young man leaped at her, leering, screaming obscenities. He had a tomahawk in his raised hand and Kateri's heart began to pound like the celebration drum.

Had she seen this brave a long time ago at the dances Karitha insisted she attend? Yes, she had seen him many times before. She had seen him with Iowerano just yesterday. Now he appeared to be ready to kill her, but why? Had Iowerano sent him?

Kateri Tekakwitha said not a word. She merely dropped her head, her chin resting upon her chest. If Iowerano wanted her dead because she had accepted the Christian faith, then she would gladly die. She would die happily for *Rawanniio*. She would give her life for the one true God.

It was as if time stood still. As she waited for the blow to fall she could hear the gentle sound of trickling water that fed the spring. She heard the birds singing, and the brave, his breath coming in excited gasps, and she waited. Nothing happened. When she raised her head she found herself looking deep into the young man's eyes. Was it fear she saw there? How could he be afraid of her? She was so thin now her tunic hung loosely on her small frame. With a thud, the tomahawk fell from the man's hand and he uttered a cry. He looked so pitiful Kateri felt sorry for him. His face contorted as if he would weep. Sucking in his breath, he turned and ran, disappearing into the thick brush.

Kateri was shaken, but she rose from the grass and began to fill the water buckets. She was deeply hurt, knowing that her family would go to such lengths to try to dissuade her from her new faith. Nothing would shake her, nothing could break her, not even death.

Kateri made no mention of the persecutions to Father de Lamberville, though the struggle continued day after day. She accepted this as part of her life, as reparation for her sins. However, the good father had told her that the sins she confessed were not transgressions at all.

She began to pray, but the weakness she felt earlier interfered with her thoughts. What she had just experienced impaired her concentration. Her communion with God had always been an easy meditation; prayers had fallen from her lips without hesitation. Now she realized her relationship with God was suffering because of the persecutions. She made up her mind to go to Father de Lamberville and unburden her heart. Perhaps the *rakeni* would tell her what to do.

She left her buckets at the spring and wearily walked to the chapel. Timidly she knocked at the side door where Father de Lamberville studied. The priest appeared surprised when he saw her. "Kateri, I was going to send for you."

"Then you know, Father?"

"I've learned of our visitors, if that's what you mean."

Kateri was puzzled. She knew nothing of visitors, but she poured out her heart to Father de Lamberville.

"Kateri, child, I suspected it, but I wasn't sure."

"I would not have told you, Father, if all these things had not kept my true heart hidden from *Rawanniio*. If even for one small moment I am apart from my Creator, then I cannot bear it. If not for that, I would have kept silent."

"Kateri," Father de Lamberville said, "God has plans for you. Chief Garonyage, Onas, and Jacob, another

Christian whom you do not know, have come to take you to the Praying Castle. Anastasia waits for you at the Mission du Sault. She heard of your suffering and she has planned your rescue."

"Anastasia knew?" Kateri asked, tears in her eyes.

"Someone from Caughnawaga brought news of your ill treatment. Anastasia worried for your safety. She sent three good Christian men whom she trusts, to bring you home."

Kateri trembled now, not from fatigue or hunger, but from relief that the torment would soon end and she would live with Christians in peace to practice her faith.

"Father, how will I leave without Iowerano finding out? He would never let me go."

Father de Lamberville's brows knit together. "Iowerano just left for Fort Orange. His trading expeditions usually take a little time. As you know, he likes to socialize with his friends there."

"God has planned it all," said Kateri, her hands folded as if in prayer. "I will go to the long house and bundle my belongings."

"No," Father de Lamberville said quickly. "You must take nothing. You must not give your aunts any reason to say you have stolen anything. Better to leave everything behind. Whatever you need will be provided for you."

"How can I thank you, Father?" Kateri hung her head in humility. "I have so much to thank you for."

"No, child. It is God who is responsible. Here. I have prepared a letter and you must give it to the good father at the Praying Castle."

Kateri took the envelope with trembling hands. She couldn't read, but she would take good care of it and deliver it as she was told.

Within a short while, Garonyage knocked on the

door and entered with a smile for Kateri, but she didn't recognize him. His long gray hair half hid his face. He had draped a fur cape across his shoulders and it hid the lower part of his face.

"Little sister," he said, "we must leave in haste. All is ready. The canoe is waiting. We will depart while Iowerano is busy at the Fort. Onas and Jacob are waiting at Big Rock. You go first and stay out of sight. I will follow."

Father de Lamberville made the sign of the cross, gave them a blessing and Kateri pulled her blanket over her head. She slipped out of the study and disappeared into the forest, hurrying to Big Rock where Onas and Jacob were waiting.

Walking close to the water's edge, but staying in the dense trees and bushes, she wandered to the designated spot. Once she ducked behind a tree when two children came prancing down a nearby path. They had been picking strawberries and each of them had a pail almost full. The juice from the berries had stained their lips and chins. They looked as if they had been painted for a celebration. As soon as their laughter died away, Kateri was on the move again. Garonyage followed closely, his arms filled with supplies.

Onas helped Kateri seat herself in the canoe of elm bark. As it moved from the shore and took Kateri away from Caughnawaga, she looked back with sadness. It was painful to leave the village she loved, but her heart sang with joy for the new life she was about to begin.

Kateri heard Onas' voice above the rush of the water. "We must make good time. We want to pass Fort Orange before Iowerano finishes his trading. When I tell you, Kateri, you must drop down onto the floor of the canoe and we'll cover you with this blanket. We cannot take any chances."

Onas kept a good lookout for Iowerano, but they didn't pass even one canoe along the way. When they neared Fort Orange, he called out, "Now, Kateri, drop down!"

She did as she was told and Onas threw a blanket over her. In the darkness she imagined seeing her stepfather on the shore outside the trading post. In her mind's eye, he looked angry. She knew that when he came home to find her gone, he would look just like that, his thin lips, a straight line, his eyes bulging in anger and disbelief. He would certainly search for her, and if he found her, he would bring her back to Caughnawaga. He would probably find it hard to believe that anyone would dare defy him to help his stepdaughter escape. Her disappearance would be something of a mystery to him, to Karitha and Arosen, and perhaps even to the entire village.

Kateri shivered beneath the warm blanket. She had never lost her fear of her uncle. She wondered what her punishment would be should he find her. She knew one thing as sure as she knew she was crouching in the bottom of the canoe, she would gladly give her life for *Rawanniio*.

Chapter Twelve

The canoe glided smoothly in the water. It made the rapids with the sureness of Mohawk ingenuity, then sped along in the quiet river again. Kateri was weary, but excited. When Onas said, "We are close to the village now," her heart began to pound so hard she could hear it beating in her ears.

She stepped from the canoe and suddenly found herself in the arms of Anastasia. The older woman's big warm embrace enveloped Kateri in a circle of love and she couldn't help herself. The tears came even though she tried with all her strength to keep them back.

"Little Sunshine," said Anastasia. "You are home! You are safely home!" Her wet cheek met the rough face of Kateri and they wept together.

There on the shore a large wooden cross had been erected to mark the Praying Castle. The Christian village had been moved twice. Now it was situated on the St. Lawrence River across from Montreal. It was called the *Mission du Sault*, which meant mission at the rapids or falls.

Kateri was comforted to see the familiar long houses, exactly like the ones at Caughnawaga, but fewer. Kateri stared in awe at the church, similar to the one she had seen at Fort Orange. The steeple was gold and it shone like a beacon in the sunlight.

The town was governed by four Indian leaders and each household was managed by an older woman who made decisions for the family. Onas and Enita lived in the long house where Kateri would make her home. Anastasia was the head of that household. It was she who made all the decisions and met the spiritual needs of the family.

The house was much like Iowerano's long house. Kateri had her own little compartment, a bench, a sleeping shelf, and an animal skin partition for privacy.

"This is where you will stay," Anastasia said as she brought Kateri to a dim corner of the smoky dwelling. "These things are for you. You will be supplied with whatever you need. There is very good trading at Ville Marie."

Kateri brought a gentle hand to a pile of soft skins. A basket of wampum and ribbons sat nearby. There were needles and stacks of bast, leather, porcupine quills and beads. "Everything I need for sewing," she said, her breath catching. "I am so grateful."

Anastasia smiled. "Your handiwork will support you, Kateri. That is, if you do not find a husband." She winked. "There are braves here, too."

Kateri looked down and shook her head. "I want only to be a Christian and worship God."

Anastasia frowned. "You are a strange one, Kateri. I will leave you now and prepare a meal. You must be hungry."

Kateri sighed. She felt peace within herself and with her surroundings. Somehow the fear that Iowerano might follow her here to the Praying Castle did not disturb her now. *Rawanniio* was guiding her.

A delicate layer of pine boughs covered with a soft deer skin composed the bed where she would sleep. A warm fur was spread over all, but resting upon the bed were new moccasins, and squares of linen. Wampum hung against the wall above the bed and there were knives and tools for scraping and carving. Already Kateri was visualizing the things she would make to help support the family.

"*Segon, skennon gowa!* Welcome!" Kateri turned to face Enita.

Enita had grown plumper, her face was radiant. "Dear sister, I am so happy to see you! I thought I would never see you again."

Enita hugged Kateri and then stood back and said. "How is our father and the family? I have prayed for them."

The mention of Iowerano, Karitha and Arosen sent a shiver through her, but Kateri said, "They are in good health. The last corn harvest was better than usual. There is enough to eat. The village has been safe."

"Thank God for that! Father de Lamberville sent bits of news from time to time." Enita hugged Kateri again. "We heard of your baptism, Kateri Tekakwitha. We were all so happy."

Kateri's face had suddenly lost its weariness. "Please take me to the chapel," she said. "I would like to offer my thanks to God there. I will tell Anastasia I will do my eating later."

The church was different than the chapel at Caughnawaga. It was different than the rough bark houses of the Christians. It was a large wooden building and on the very top a gilded cross shone in the bright sun.

Kateri opened the door slowly and entered the dark chapel. The scent of candle wax and incense greeted her. She was alone, alone with the one true God.

"Oh, *Rawanniio*," she whispered, "I know you better now and I shall come to know you better still. I love you more than life itself. You are in my heart forever."

Shadows from the trees outside fell upon the windows and the church grew darker. Still Kateri knelt at the altar, reflecting upon the goodness of God. Only the clang of the bells that sounded the *Angelus* roused Kateri, not the emptiness of hunger. Reluctantly she left the chapel.

It was almost twilight. She heard a voice call out, "Tekakwitha! Welcome." Father Fremin was standing in the waning sun with Father Cholenec and Father Chauchetiere.

"Fathers," he said, "this is Kateri Tekakwitha." He turned back to Kateri. "How you have grown, little one. You were a child when you served the priests in the house of Iowerano."

Kateri nodded and smiled. "This is for you from Father de Lamberville," she said, removing the letter from a pocket on her tunic.

Father Fremin read the letter and passed it to the other two priests. They exchanged knowing glances and then Father Fremin folded it and tucked it under his arm. "As soon as you are settled, Kateri, Father Cholenec will give you instructions for First Communion."

Kateri Tekakwitha took a little breath and held it. The joy in her heart spread across her face in a smile. She crossed her arms against her chest and bowed her head. "God is so good to me. How could I ever ask for anything more?"

"Go with God, Kateri," Father Fremin said, and Tekakwitha hurried home.

Anastasia's hot meal of venison, beans, corn, and bear grease brought Kateri's strength rushing back. She was flushed with happiness and gratitude. Everyone at the Praying Castle welcomed her. Not one curse did she hear, not one bad look did she receive, not one voice was raised in anger.

The long house was dim and smoky. This had never bothered the Indians, but for many years and even now, smoke made Kateri's eyes water. She was forced to close them for long periods. The crackling of the fire and the muffled conversation between Onas and Enita were the only sounds. The children were fast asleep. Odors from the evening meal mingled with the smoke and night came. Kateri had to pinch herself to make sure she wasn't dreaming. Tomorrow she would be up before dawn for Mass, then she would receive instructions in the faith. After that she would attend to household chores, work in the fields and in her spare time she would sew.

She said her prayers and snuggled into the warm bed. With a rush of excitement she looked forward to her First Communion. A new kind of life was just unfolding.

Chapter Thirteen

Kateri's days were filled with duties, instructions in the faith, and worship. It seemed as if Christmas would never come, so anxious was she to make her First Communion.

Anastasia and Kateri Tekakwitha were inseparable. When the villagers saw one, the other was nearby. The older woman's duty was to instruct her household in spiritual matters and Kateri was eager to learn.

"I tell you, Kateri," Anastasia said often, "it is wrong to adorn oneself. Our Savior had no adornment. He came into the world with nothing. It is a great sin that some of us choose to wear the decorations of the world. Each of us should do penance for our sins."

"I know you are right," Kateri answered. "I have worn wampum in the past and it pains me now to think of it."

The older woman nodded. "I am pleased that you recognize your failings. You are a good Christian."

But that wasn't the end of it. Kateri laid awake nights thinking of the many times she wore the decorations her aunts had insisted upon and she wept remembering. She chastised herself for the times spent at the festivals when she wore her best tunic and leggings.

She had perfected her sewing and the finished items brought in enough money to supply her with all that she needed. However, Kateri chose to repay Onas and his family for their hospitality and kept little for herself.

A few days before Christmas the first heavy snow of the season fell upon the Praying Castle. The long houses, the church, the tall wooden cross on the shore, the trees and the foot paths, all were covered with a white blanket. Anastasia had laid aside a wool veil, white as the snow, for Kateri Tekakwitha to wear at her First Communion.

"It is fitting that you wear wampum this time, Kateri," she said. "You will be giving honor to the Lord in the Sacrament of Holy Communion."

"No," answered Kateri in that gentle but determined voice. Anastasia had come to recognize the tone as being final in any discussion. "Our Lord came into the world with nothing and he left with nothing. I choose to wear only the veil, not the wampum." Anastasia's brow wrinkled and her eyebrows knit together, but she said nothing.

The women had decorated the church with pine boughs and red berries, rich beaver pelts and furs. The good fathers had taught carols to the children in their own language. As Kateri approached the altar they sang, their voices as sweet as angels. It was as if the cherubim had descended from heaven to sing at Kateri Tekakwitha's First Communion.

The aura of her first confession remained with her. As she knelt to receive the Body and Blood of Christ, tears streamed down her cheeks. She bowed her head and knelt transfixed, for she believed that God dwelled within her. Never had she known such perfect happiness.

Mass ended. One by one the people quietly left the church, all but Kateri. She could not bear to leave. Winter would be long. She would not be allowed to partake of communion again until Easter. That was the custom.

The cold winds, spawned in the north, blew off the river and during the night everything froze. The ice on the St. Lawrence was thick enough to walk on, and the time had come for the winter hunt to begin.

Kateri longed to stay at home where Mass would be celebrated daily. But only the elderly and the ill persons would be allowed to stay. The priests would tend to those who remained. Kateri wished with all her heart to be close to the church and the tabernacle within, but she was needed on the trail. Willingly she accompanied Onas, Enita and their children.

One dreary morning when the sky was leaden gray and the snow was falling, the hunting party left the Sault and trudged into the depths of the snowy forest. Kateri looked back at the church and raised her eyes to the gold cross. She turned back again and again until the golden cross was out of sight. She pulled her thin blanket tighter, bowed her head, and followed the rest.

In the afternoon the group stopped in a clearing. It was time to make camp. All hands were needed and Kateri helped Enita and the women gather pine boughs for the temporary shelter. Onas built a framework and piled the pine brush around it. Skins were spread over all, and though the dwelling was not as snug as the long house, it made a cozy temporary home. The women would spend much of their time outdoors, preparing meat and tanning hides. While the men were away on the hunt, the women would enjoy some leisure, telling of past events, gossiping and visiting. When the men

returned, too exhausted to do anything but sleep, the work of the women began.

Kateri missed the church at the Praying Castle. Sometimes, when she knew her absence wouldn't be noticed, she slipped away to the woods and said her prayers. She knelt in the snow until her legs were so numb with cold she could hardly walk. She lashed two pieces of wood together and made a rude cross. She hadn't known the meaning of the symbol the first time she carved one so long ago. Now she knew and she wept when she thought of Christ and his agony. She loved the one true God with her whole heart and her whole mind and she wept, too, for the time when she hadn't known him.

When Kateri returned to camp, a blustering wind whipped the frame house, whistling through the cracks and down the smoke hole. The women huddled inside, praying their men would come home safely.

"The men will be late," Enita said. "The wind will slow them down."

"They will be too tired to eat," Seceweda said, "but we'll leave *sagamite* and beans in the pot for them anyway."

It grew dark earlier than usual and the women bedded down around the fire. They drew what little warmth they could from the cookfire.

When Kateri awakened, she found Seceweda staring down at her, glowering, both hands planted on her wide hips. Kateri turned and saw Seceweda's husband, Louis, asleep beside her. The men had come home, exhausted from the hunt, and in the darkness they dropped down to sleep anywhere. But the look in Seceweda's eyes told Kateri there was suspicion in her heart. Kateri jumped up, smoothed her hair, draped her blanket over her head and left the house.

Enita was already working, carving the meat from a

large moose and Kateri began to help her. The wind had died during the night. Now the sun lit the snow and the ground sparkled like a mass of tiny jewels. The blood from the slain animal made small dark rivulets in the trampled snow.

"Watch out for Seceweda," Enita said. "Stay out of Louis' way. She is jealous, that one."

"I have done nothing wrong," Kateri said simply. "I want the company of no man."

"Just remember what I said," Enita whispered. "Stay out of her husband's way."

The work lasted for more than four days, but finally the meat had been prepared and the skins hung between trees or over branches. Onas announced that soon they would return to the village. Kateri smiled when she heard that. She wanted more than anything to go back to the church called St. Xavier and to the tall cross on the shore.

The day before the hunting party planned their return to the Praying Castle the women sat in the sun and repaired moccasins, shirts and tunics. The weather was cold, but warmer than in the past and the sun felt good on Kateri's shoulders. The women chattered, gossip on their tongues. Kateri asked, "Do any of you know the new hymn Father Fremin taught us? Sing it with me."

The small group of noisy women found themselves singing with Kateri, praising God the father and forgetting the taletelling. Kateri smiled. Her voice could be heard a little above all the others.

The hymn was over and Kateri was about to remind the women of another hymn when Louis came out to the group of women. He faced Kateri and smiled. "Would you be so kind as to sew a part of the canoe I am making? It is a difficult task and you are best when it comes to the needle."

Kateri, always happy and willing to help and without thinking, said, "I will gladly sew whatever you wish."

Seceweda sucked in her breath and her nostrils flared. Kateri realized too late that this jealous women saw something evil in her answer.

It was time to return to the Sault and Kateri was happier. Some members of the party returned in canoes laden with dried meat, furs, and skins. Kateri was part of the band that trudged back on tired feet. When she caught sight of the gold cross on the steeple she began to run. Oh, it was so good to be home, so good to be back to worship at Mass. She hurried to the chapel and knelt at the altar. "Thank you God for a good hunt and for bringing us back safely. I have missed your presence in the tabernacle, yet I know you were with me the whole time away. I am undeserving of your love, good Jesus, but I know you love me, will always love me, as I will always love you."

Kateri remained in the cold, unheated chapel, her hands folded, her head bowed. She stayed until the shadows fell and the light no longer came through the windows. Only then did she get up and return home. But as she quietly left the chapel, she saw Seceweda wrapping at the door of Father Fremin's study. The door opened and Kateri heard Father Fremin say, "Welcome home from the hunt, Seceweda. You look upset. Is something wrong?"

"I must speak to you Father," Seceweda said. "Something happened on the hunt. I must discuss it with you."

"Come in, child, come in," said Father Fremin. "Tell me what is troubling you."

The door closed and Kateri stood on the steps of the chapel feeling very alone and very sad.

Chapter Fourteen

Kateri stared at the calendar on the wall above Father Fremin's head. It pictured Mary, the mother of God. She wore a blue head covering and Kateri was surprised that it looked much like her own.

"Catherine," Father Fremin said. "I want you to confess to me if you have committed a sin on the hunting trip. That is why I asked you to come. I am here to help you."

Tears shone in Kateri's dark eyes. She swallowed with difficulty, smothering the suffering she was trying very hard to keep within. "I have done nothing wrong, Father."

Father Fremin sighed. Silence followed Kateri's statement. She had answered as best she could. Suddenly her shoulders shook and she wept, covering her face with her hands. "I have done nothing wrong," she repeated.

"I know you well, little Catherine. I know you would tell me if you had sinned. I am sorry, but I had to ask you. That is my duty as a priest. I must watch over my flock of Christians. You have been accused of mischief, but if you say it is not true, then I believe you."

Kateri lowered her head. "Thank you, Father. I have done nothing wrong."

Father Fremin smiled. "Dry your eyes, little one. Father De Lamberville, in the letter you delivered, wrote that your soul is very close to the Lord. He said that through our spiritual guidance we would soon realize what a jewel we have. We recognize that, Kateri. Go with God."

Father Fremin made the sign of the cross in blessing and Kateri quietly left his study. But her heart was broken. To be accused of desiring a woman's husband was unthinkable. She, Kateri, had no desire for a husband, not her own and not any other.

She walked slowly back to the long house. She was happy to be home, happy to be in the company of Anastasia again, but the accusations, the blame, weighed heavily. Did she imagine that Anastasia's bright eyes were clouded with an accusatory look? Did she imagine a faint aloofness in her smile? The darkness of the long house seemed overpowering after the walk in the bright sun and there was something in Anastasia's voice that frightened Kateri.

As the days went by, Anastasia stayed close to the side of Kateri Tekakwitha. It had been her duty to tutor the girl in the faith and she was determined to do it well.

"Kateri," she said one day as she and Kateri gathered wild berries, "we must all do more penance for our sins. None of us is worthy in the eyes of God. We must work to make ourselves holy."

"Yes, Anastasia," Kateri answered. "I am not worthy to set foot inside the chapel, poor sinner that I have been. I must do what is pleasing to God. I must try to erase my sins by doing penance. That is the only way to attain the kingdom of God."

Anastasia nodded and wiped the sweat from her round face with her hand. "I know you understand, child."

Anastasia leaned closer. "We must not only do penance for our own sins, but we must do penance for our poor brothers and sisters who have not yet been converted." She looked at Kateri out of the corner of her eye. "We are all guilty, Kateri. We are all sinners."

Kateri looked into the bucket of luscious berries. They were red and ripe and smelled sweetly. It would have been so wonderful to pop a handful into her mouth. She was thirsty and hungry. But no, to deny herself was to do penance. She stifled the desire and instead said a silent prayer as she searched for more berries.

That night, she lay awake listening to the wind that rifled the bark of the long house. She heard the whisperings of Enita and Onas, and Anastasia's heavy breathing. Anastasia's words came back to her again and again, like the pounding rain on the roof of the long house during a lengthy storm. Anastasia was right. Penance was the only way to atone for sin. She could not be pleasing to God until she did penance. She promised herself she would find many ways to make amends, many kinds of sacrifices to make herself more pleasing to God. But she knew that she must do it privately.

Before the sun rose the next morning Kateri was on the path to the woods where she would take another direction, one not often used by the villagers. It was just dawning when she found the spot where she planned to make her own place of prayer. She took out her knife and began to carve a cross on the trunk of a great tree. The fury of the wind whipped her hair against her face and removed the blanket from her head and shoulders. Freezing rain pelted her body. With stiff fingers, she continued to carve the cross and when she was finished she stood back, knelt on the cold ground and began to pray. She recited every prayer she had ever learned. Then she said each one again and again. By the time she prepared to leave, her legs were like chunks of ice and she couldn't feel her toes. Only then did she return to the village, happy from her communion with God, but discontented with her inadequate penance. She began to devise more austere ways of fulfilling her promise to repent.

Lent began and the whole village looked forward to Easter. On Wednesdays and Fridays Kateri fasted, She brought the food she denied herself to the poor and the sick. For the purpose of perfecting her penance, she thought of ways to make sleeping less pleasurable. She put sharp rocks in her bed and secretly sprinkled ashes on her food to make it less palatable. She believed she must deny her body, she must do these things for *Rawanniio* to show him perfect love.

Anastasia frowned when she noticed Kateri's intense fastings. The girl had become so thin and pale.

"All things in balance, Kateri. Do not do penance that will bring harm to you. God would not want that."

But it was Anastasia's own advice in the past that awakened Kateri to the guilt of sin. Because of Anastasia's admonishings, Kateri wept in seclusion for the times when she had adorned herself with wampum.

Kateri answered, "I must show God how much I love him. I must also offer my sufferings for those of my people who do not yet know him."

Anastasia shook her head. Kateri had the strength and courage of her Mohawk heritage. Nothing would dissuade her once she had made up her mind.

In preparation for Easter Sunday, the fathers taught the children hymns in the language of the Iroquois. Kateri spent hours on her knees in church and thrilled to

the sweet voices of the children who practiced. Her knees hurt, her legs became numb. Whenever she could leave the village unnoticed, she would hurry off to her special place of prayer. She remained dissatisfied with her penances, believing they were inadequate. Only penance would save her soul and help her people to come to know the one true God.

Anastasia noticed Kateri's absences and wondered about them. She was sure the girl spent her time in prayer and that was as it should be. But Kateri was driven by a mysterious compulsion to do more severe penance.

The church on Easter Sunday was decorated with wild flowers. Mass was offered early in the morning and the entire village took part. The little wooden church was crowded with Christians, so many they could hardly be housed. A new church, made of stone had been started close by. It was almost finished and the building was the pride of the village.

On this Sunday, Kateri, for the second time, was allowed to receive communion and she came away from the altar rail with her face in her hands, her shoulders shaking. She wept for joy to receive the one true God, *Rawanniio*, to whom she had dedicated her life.

Anastasia turned to view Kateri. The girl was sobbing quietly and the old woman moved back. There was something about this girl whom she loved as a daughter that was like no one else. Anastasia reflected upon the day Kateri Tekakwitha was born and the days and years that followed. Within this frail human creature, there seemed to dwell a mysterious holiness that set her apart from all the rest. Within this small resolute girl, a heroic spirit seemed to have made its home and Anastasia was bewildered.

The cloud of incense had gradually disappeared,

but the scent of frankincense hung in the air and mingled with the smell of candle wax. One by one the people shuffled out of the dark church. Anastasia gently tapped Kateri on the shoulder. "Come, Kateri, it is time to go home. We must prepare our feast for the fathers."

Kateri roused herself, looked up and smiled. "In my remaining days I must do whatever is most pleasing to God."

Anastasia gazed upon Kateri with wonder. Her words were unsettling.

Chapter Fifteen

Kateri Tekakwitha was over twenty years old and still not married. Anastasia looked up from her sewing and shook her head. "Kateri, it is for your own good that you marry. Who will take care of you when you are older? I will not be around forever. I would be so..." Kateri paused and let the needle slide from the skin. "Never will I marry, Mother, though I know it is a right and good state for Christians. I cannot explain it. This is hard to say." She let the soft skin fall to her lap. "My spouse is not man. He is God."

Anastasia marveled at the girl's expression whenever she mentioned the name of God. Should I leave her alone? she thought. Is it right to interfere with such a spiritual person as Kateri? But she turned away, puzzled. This was not a girl she understood. And was this a girl she ought to change?

Kateri put her sewing aside and reached for her blanket. It was time for her afternoon devotions. As she stepped outside, a gentle breeze touched her face. The bright sun still affected her eyesight unfavorably and she drew the covering over her forehead to shade her eyes.

The new stone church was finished except for a few details and Kateri was drawn to the building. The interior was cool and dim. It smelled of fresh lumber and paint. She stood in the aisle, staring at the new pews, the communion rail and the beautiful hand-carved altar. The stations of the cross, which helped her recall the passion of Christ, were all in place. The only sound she heard was the tap-tapping of a hammer one of the workmen was using to complete some last minute task.

She didn't need to turn around to know that someone was standing in the aisle behind her. The human presence was suddenly comforting, as if an angel had come to keep her company. She turned to see this angel, this friend.

"This is such a beautiful church," a woman's voice said softly. Kateri recognized the language as that belonging to the Oneida Indians and she understood the words.

"Yes," she answered, "but it is not this building of wood and stone where God most loves to dwell. It is in our hearts where he longs to be. And I am not deserving to worship here."

The woman's expression showed surprise. "You are good. I know you are good. I want to be your friend."

Kateri warmed at the words this new Christian spoke. In the woman's eyes she saw a kinship, a closeness that only God could have sent. "I *am* your friend," she answered.

"I am Therese Tegaiagonta," the woman said.

"And I am Kateri Tekakwitha."

The woman's lips parted in surprise. "I have heard of you," she said. "You are the good Christian from Caughnawaga. You have earned the love and respect of many of our people."

"I am not deserving," Kateri said softly. "I am not deserving."

"Come," said Therese. "Let us walk down to the cross by the shore. It is such a beautiful place, a good place to pray."

The two of them went down to the shore and sat beneath the tall wooden cross. They had so much to tell each other, so much to share. Therese Tegaiagonta spoke without hesitation.

"Father Bruyas baptized me," she said, "but I almost lost my Christian faith. I took the whiskey and behaved badly. For this I will be sorry all the rest of my life."

Kateri put her hand on the woman's shoulder. "God will forgive you if you are truly sorry. And there is no whiskey here at the Praying Castle."

"I was married," she said, choking back tears. "I lost my husband and two children. I will never marry again. I have come to the Sault to lead a good Christian life. I want to dedicate my life to God."

Kateri put her arm around Therese. "You have come to the right place," she said. "Together we will show God how much we love him. Together we will do penance and attain a perfect love of God."

"I have so much to repent," Therese said, tears streaming down her cheeks. "I have committed many sins. Sometimes I cannot bear to think of them."

"None of us is worthy," answered Kateri. "Penance will make us greater in the eyes of God."

Therese dried her eyes with her fingers and smiled. "Let us pray here, beneath this cross. This is the beginning of a new life for me."

Kateri could hardly wait to tell Anastasia about Therese. She could not explain the kinship she felt with this new Christian. She recognized the friendship as a gift from God, as heaven-sent. *Rawanniio* knew the emptiness of her worldly being. All of her life she had no one with which she could share her every thought, no one who would understand her innermost feelings. Now Therese had come to be her companion and it was as if Kateri had known Therese all of her life.

"Yes," Anastasia said when Kateri came home excited and happy. "I met the young woman, a fine Onieda who has had a bad time of it. I liked her the moment I met her."

"As soon as Therese has had time to make moccasins and belts, she and I will go with the other women to the Ville Marie, (Montreal) to trade and sell our wares. And when we work together we will pray."

Anastasia smiled. It was good to see Kateri so happy. The years wore heavily on the old woman. Ordinary tasks were becoming too difficult. These she left to Kateri and Enita. Lately she had spent less and less time in Kateri's company. And, she thought, Kateri should have a young companion to pass the time with, a good Christian woman who knew the faith and practiced it well.

Kateri's heart glowed with new devotion. She would seek a perfect love for *Rawanniio*. That was Therese's wish as well. Together, like sisters, they would help each other achieve that love.

In the weeks that followed, Kateri and Therese spent much of their time making trading items to take to Ville Marie. They made blankets of deerskin, belts and moccasins encrusted with glass beads. Kateri embroidered skins and carved wooden bowls and spoons. Sometimes they prayed while they worked. Other times they prayed beneath the tall wooden cross on the shore of the Sault or in the quiet of the new church. But Kateri believed that to have perfect love for God a person must do *great* penance.

She spent many sleepless hours thinking about how best to do penance. She came to the conclusion that it wasn't enough to go without food and water. She believed now that persons must suffer great pain to atone for their sins. She discussed this with Therese who agreed. They must suffer great pain to atone for their sins.

The first trip Kateri and Therese made to Ville Marie was in 1678. They joined a group of women who, like themselves, wanted to trade or sell their handiwork to French settlers.

The canoe that carried Therese, Kateri and a small group of women along with their trading items, crossed the wide river. It beached on the mossy banks. French guns were pointed toward the river, but posed no threat to the Christian Indians. Kateri, awed by the buildings, pointed to the governor's mansion, the mills, the brewery and the high walls that ringed the buildings. She was drawn to a small chapel where the chanting of women's voices drifted from the open windows.

"What does it mean?" asked Kateri, peering at a group of women hidden behind a wooden grate.

"They call themselves nuns," a companion answered. "They live together in one building. They never marry, but pray, teach, and tend the sick. They call the hospital the Hotel Dieu."

Kateri was fascinated. "Come, Therese," she said, "we must learn more about this."

Kateri's companions went directly to the marketplace to barter and sell their wares. Kateri and Therese visited the small chapel and then asked permission to enter the Hotel Dieu.

Kateri couldn't believe her eyes. The women who were tending the sick colonists were all dressed alike. They wore long black dresses and strange three pointed caps that were white and stiff. Their clothing was clean, but patched and threadbare. Every one of the women smiled!

A plump nun with a round pink face escorted Kateri and Therese. She showed them the hospital, the school and the convent of Notre Dame. Kateri learned, with great satisfaction that these quiet, happy nuns lived their lives apart from the world and remained unmarried. They left comfortable, often wealthy homes in France to minister to the colonists. They led lives of sacrifice, sharing the danger and hardships of New France.

"They are much like the *rakeni*," Kateri told Therese later. "The blackrobes never marry. They devote their lives to God through prayer and helping people. That is a perfect life. We, too, will live a perfect life in a convent we will build ourselves."

"We need the advice of an older, experienced woman who thinks as we do," said Therese. "I know the one. Her name is Marie Skarichions. I will ask her help."

The next morning, Kateri, Therese, and Marie met in the shadow of the tall wooden cross on the shore to discuss the community they wished to form.

"Where will we build our convent?" asked Therese.

Kateri looked out across the river to the Island of the Herons. "There!" she said pointing excitedly. "That will be the place to build our prayer lodge. There we can devote our lives to God, away from distraction where we can pray and give God perfect love."

"Ah," said Marie. "Before we do anything we must first talk to Father Fremin. We must have his permission and advice."

Kateri nodded. "Yes, we must be obedient to the authority of the mission father. We will do nothing until we speak to him."

But in her mind, Kateri laid her plans. It would be a

wonderful community. She could see the long house they would build. She could even see the gardens behind it and the trees and flowers that surrounded it. With all her heart she wished it would become a reality.

Chapter Sixteen

Kateri knocked timidly at the door of Father Fremin's study. She had always been shy, but to ask permission to build a convent on the Island of the Herons suddenly seemed a strange thing to do. There she was, a poor uneducated Indian, trying to behave like the beautiful, wonderful nuns she met at the convent of Notre Dame.

Inside the study, she sat on the edge of a chair and drew her blanket closer. "I have come, Father, to ask your advice."

Father Fremin leaned forward. "What do you ask?"

"I ask...." She paused, seeming to lose courage; finding the right words stretched beyond her thought. "I ask..." she repeated. "I ask that I, Therese and Marie Skarichions be allowed to build a convent."

The lines around Father Fremin's eyes deepened and he put his hands to his mouth to suppress a chuckle.

"Where do you propose to build this convent?"

Kateri became animated and she thrust her hand out pointing in the direction of the Island of the Herons.

Her timid voice grew louder. "The most beautiful place, Father. The Island of the Herons!"

Father Fremin chuckled unrestrainedly. "Oh, Kateri," he said. "That cannot possibly be. You are new to the faith and the Island of the Herons is too far from the village. You would be disturbed by the young men coming and going to Ville Marie. They travel that route. It is out of the question. Out of the question!"

Kateri's innocent expression, her surprise at his words, gave the priest a sudden sense of accountability. "You are better served in the house of Onas." he said gently. "You are a faithful good Christian. Continue as you are."

"But Father," Kateri's voice was persistent, "I wish never to marry."

Father Fremin paused. "God leaves every Christian free to marry or not as he chooses, Catherine. Whether you marry or not is your choice. The holy state of matrimony is what God wishes for most people, but it is not for everyone."

Kateri rose from her chair and thanked the priest. His words were reasonable, and long ago she had made good friends with obedience. She would bring the priest's message to her two companions and attempt to console them.

Therese and Marie and Kateri were disappointed. But they discussed their plans and Father Fremin's words. Then decided to drop the matter. They would find a way to attain perfect love for God without founding a convent.

Enita heard of the thwarted plans and she discussed them with Anastasia.

"It is not right, Mother, that Kateri remains unmarried. Old age awaits Onas and we need a young hunter to bring food to the cabin. Kateri needs a husband. She may not always have you or Onas and I. What would become of her? I know she refused a pagan brave in the past, but here she could have the finest Christian husband. Everyone loves Kateri."

Anastasia agreed. "Of course you are right, Enita. Have you noticed that she does not oil her hair. She cares little about her appearance. Her clothes are old and worn. We must speak to her."

When Kateri entered the long house, Anastasia and Enita sat her down on one of the low benches. They began to pressure her, making all the arguments they could think of in favor of her marrying.

Kateri shook her head, but since she owed much to Anastasia and Enita she listened politely. These good women deserved respect.

"I thank both of you for your concern for my welfare. But you must not worry, my needs are small. I will give the matter consideration. That is all."

Anastasia sighed with relief. "There is hope, Enita. At least Kateri didn't refuse the proposition altogether."

Kateri did give the matter consideration and the more she thought about it the more disturbed she became. Perhaps, she thought, Father Cholenec could tell her how she might convince her sister and Anastasia that she wanted no part of marriage.

Father Cholenec listened patiently, his folded hands resting on the rude desk. "You know, Kateri, there are many fine Christian men who would be happy to marry you and provide for you. Marriage is a natural state. God wants that for most people. Have you thought the matter through?"

"Ah, Father," she answered, "I am not any longer my own. I have given myself to Jesus Christ. He is my Master. I am not afraid of poverty. I have few needs. I fear nothing."

Father Cholenec pondered the matter, scratching his head for an apt reply. He could think of none and he said, "Go, Kateri. God will provide the answer in due time."

Anastasia, resentful that Kateri did not take her advice, determined to change the girl's mind. She decided to go to Father Cholenec herself. Perhaps he would talk some sense into the girl.

Father Cholenec listened patiently to Anastasia's railings and complaints. Then he rubbed his chin and said softly, "Leave the girl alone. She has been through enough. You must let her decide for herself. I have noticed, as surely you must have, that Kateri's health has weakened. We must support her in her beliefs and put as little strain on her as possible. Her heart and soul belong to God."

Anastasia went home chastised. Yes, she had noticed how thin and pale Kateri Tekakwitha had become. But she had been too busy thinking of other matters and ignored the problem at hand. And if God approved of Kateri's decision then who was she to argue?

"Forgive me, Kateri," she said, when Kateri came in from the fields, weary and spent. "I have worried about things that were not most important. You have become feeble and I have let it pass. Please forgive me."

Kateri smiled. "It is nothing, Anastasia. Nothing to be concerned about. If I am pleasing in the eyes of God, then I desire nothing more. I live for him. There is nothing to forgive."

But in private, Anastasia wept to think that she had caused Kateri any anguish and had allowed her to ruin her health.

Once again the time of the winter hunt was near. Anastasia promised herself that she would tend to the girl's welfare, make sure she ate regularly and enough.

The mountain air would do her good. She would come home plump and healthy.

Kateri declined to go along with the family party. She had promised herself that never again would she go on the winter hunt. She remained in the village, subsisting only on Indian corn. The food supply had been depleted, but she had disciplined herself for many years. Severe fasts were something she did regularly. She wore rosary beads around her neck and she prayed, often in the cold of the forest, or in the drafty silence of the long house. Her thoughts went back to the sisters at the Hotel Dieu. After repeatedly questioning the priests, she came to the conclusion that these women were Christian virgins who had dedicated their lives to God. They had taken the vow of chastity, the promise that they would never marry. Kateri wanted to be like them.

The snow fell softly on the deserted Mission du Sault where Kateri's small moccasins made a single trail to the chapel in the quiet afternoon. She had to speak to Father Cholenec.

"What is troubling you, child?" he asked when he saw her at his door.

The blue blanket she wore now in place of the red one so common to all the girls and women, had shielded her face from the falling snow. The blanket was thin and worn and her tunic was old. Only her moccasins were new. She had stitched these because the old ones were falling off her feet.

She spoke with great urgency. "Father, I want to take the vow of virginity. I must consecrate myself to God while there is still time. It is more important to me than life."

Father Cholenec's lower lip parted from his thick mustache. "Kateri, that is something to which I cannot give my consent. You are a model for all the women

here, but you must think seriously about taking a vow."

"I have thought about it, Father. I am sure that is what I want to do. I want to be like the nuns at the Hotel Dieu. I do not wish to go there. I do not know how to read or write. I wish to remain here with my own people, but I want to take the vow."

Father Cholenec scratched his head. This wonderful girl never failed to surprise him. But he must caution her to wait, to think about it some more.

Kateri was determined. Long had she thought about taking the vow and she had not changed her mind. On March 25th, 1679, Kateri took the vow of chastity. No longer would she be bothered by well-intentioned matchmakers. She was *Rawanniio's* bride and she would live her life for him.

Chapter Seventeen

Therese and Kateri found a deserted cabin not far from the village. A Frenchman, a trapper, had abandoned it years ago and the building had been ravaged by the elements. Though the place had a hearth, Kateri and Therese prayed in the unheated cabin, even in the coldest weather. They knelt on the hard earthen floor when snow drifted in from the windows and doorway. Here they worshipped and performed severe penances. Every Saturday afternoon before confession they came to pray. They recited the rosary and every prayer they knew, then repeated each again and again. Kateri's Mohawk heritage had prepared her to suffer and endure and she did not find it difficult to bear great physical pain. She was happy to offer sacrifices to *Rawanniio*. Therese, a fervent follower of Kateri, an Oneida with similar training, imitated her noble friend. They confessed their sins to each other and wept for having offended God. But after each session of atonement they left the cabin with joy in their hearts.

"Therese," Kateri said one day in tears, "there were

times when my aunts insisted I work in the fields on Sunday and I was afraid of them and I went. I am so sorry for that. I must atone for those sins."

"You could not help yourself, dear Kateri. Do not blame yourself."

"I must. I lacked courage. I was weak. I feared death more than sin. I am so sorry, so sorry for that."

"God forgives all sins," replied Therese.

Kateri was not consoled. "Our people endured tortures with pride. I must endure torture in a spirit of atonement." She began to weep, and as she knelt on the earth floor, Therese realized with shock that Kateri had impaired her health with fastings and heroic penances. It frightened her.

Kateri was usually in her cabin or in church. Whenever she was needed she was always ready to help. She made five visits each day to the chapel and nothing kept her from that practice, even on days when she was not well. When she could, she tended the elderly and ill.

Her health continued to fail. She became weaker each day. Anastasia observed with alarm that she ate nothing on Wednesdays and Saturdays. Kateri tried not to draw attention to her actions. However, when Anastasia insisted that she must temper her fasts, Kateri resumed the practice of putting ashes in her food. Often she took over the responsibilities of other women whenever she could find an excuse, even when she was so tired she struggled to stand. She drove herself, denied herself, but she did this so discretely and gently that most people were not aware that it was happening.

Again Anastasia admonished her charge. "Kateri, you must stop the penances, stop the sacrifices. You will only kill yourself."

Kateri answered, "Certainly Christ upon the cross suffered more than I. My suffering is nothing by comparison."

But as the year wore on, Kateri's health continued to fail. She had to support herself against the pews when she went to church. When she knelt she often had difficulty getting up. Still, when she was able to get away by herself, she walked upon the ice or waded in the snow barefooted. She placed thorns in her bed and suffered the painful barbs joyfully the whole night. She grew pale and the skin on her face was drawn tightly over her bones. Soon she became so weak she was forced to retire to her bed.

Chapter Eighteen

Lent 1680

Father Cholenec, aware that Kateri was losing strength, brought a group of children to visit her.

"You need to rest from the constant praying," he said. "I will give the children their lessons and you may listen without tiring yourself."

With pictures, he described Sacred Scripture. Though Kateri was too weak to move, she questioned the blackrobe about many things. Father Cholenec explained the lessons carefully and the children, as well as Kateri, understood more clearly. When the session was over, the children sang hymns and Mohawk songs Kateri remembered from childhood. She smiled as she lay back against the soft skins. "Please, Father, bring the children back tomorrow. I have enjoyed their visit."

"I will, Kateri," Father Cholenec answered. "They enjoyed the visit as much as you did."

Kateri grew weaker each day. All through Lent the children received their lessons beside her bed. Her voice became almost a whisper and Anastasia hovered in the shadows watchful and silent.

Therese Tegaiagonta had to join the other women in the fields, but whenever she could, she came to Kateri's bedside. The two friends prayed together, only now Kateri's voice was nearly silent, her lips barely moving. Therese, frightened at the thought of losing her, prayed more fervently. She offered more penances to God that he might make Kateri strong again.

Since the beginning of Lent, Kateri had been too weak to go to the chapel. During all this time she hadn't been able to receive Holy Communion. On Tuesday of Holy Week Father Fremin paid Kateri a visit.

In a voice that was barely a whisper she asked, "Father, is it true what they say? Am I going to die?" She smiled. "I will soon see *Rawanniio's* face, will I not?"

Father Cholenec tried to speak, but bit his lip and closed his eyes for a moment.

"I think you will see *Rawanniio* soon, Kateri."

Her face became radiant at the reply. "I will be happy to leave," she said, "but first I want to receive the Blessed Sacrament."

The priest brought both hands together in a gesture of prayer and lifted them to his lips. He seemed to be pondering something.

"It has always been the custom for the sick and the dying to be brought to the church to receive the Lord's Supper, but you are too weak. I will talk to the fathers. We must make an exception for you. We will bring the Blessed Sacrament to you."

An expression of pure happiness spread across Kateri's face. "Now I will die happily."

The sun lit the path to Kateri's long house on this early spring day. Father Cholenec, followed by a troop of men, women and children, brought the Blessed Sacrament to Kateri. The people waited outside the door. Some knelt, some prayed, some stood silently. All grieved for Kateri who was dying.

Inside the dim smoky house, friends and family crowded around Kateri's bedside. Some whispered and some hung back in silence. Anastasia wiped tears from her eyes. Enita stood next to her, her head bowed, her hands folded. Therese and Marie Skarichions huddled close to each other, unwilling to accept the fate of their friend. These were people Kateri knew and loved. All wanted to be with her to the end.

Kateri received the Blessed Sacrament, her eyes closed, a smile on her lips. Those who had waited outside now joined in prayer. One by one they came and went, anxious to see Kateri one last time.

Kateri's face, pale as candle wax, wore a sweet, peaceful expression. She lay back upon the bed so still. Father Cholenec prepared to administer the last rites. But Kateri rallied, opened her eyes and whispered, "It is not time yet Father, not yet time."

Therese Tegaiagonta remained at Kateri's bedside throughout the evening. Her heart breaking for her dear friend, she kept her vigil, weeping. She forced herself to shed her tears without sound so that Kateri would not be disturbed.

Kateri opened her eyes and smiled. "I know very well, my sister, what I am saying. I know the place from which you came, and I know what you were doing there. Take courage! You may be sure that you are pleasing in the eyes of God, and I will help you more when I am with him."

Therese was startled by the words. "Kateri, you know all about me, even that which I never told you! In some mysterious way you know my whole life. My little soul-sister, I love you. I want to be with you to the last. I

must work tomorrow and I am afraid you will die while I am away."

"You may go to the field, Therese; do not fear. You will be back in time."

In the morning, Enita came to Kateri and expressed the same fear. "We must work in the fields. Please ask God not to let you die while we are away. We want to be with you at the end."

"On your return, you will find me still living." And when the women returned from the fields, they found Kateri still alive.

But the spirit, the soul of Kateri, was slipping away ever so slowly, like a gossamer veil falling softly to earth. She received the last rites of the Catholic Church and Enita sent for Therese. The words that fell from Kateri's lips were hardly audible. Therese leaned closer.

"I leave you," said Kateri. "I am going to die. I will love you in heaven...."

Kateri reached for her crucifix and brought it to her lips. Her expression was one of pure bliss. "I love you, Jesus," she whispered and then closed her eyes.

Kateri Tekakwitha died on Wednesday, April 17, 1680. She was twenty-four years old. Her life and death had a profound effect on everyone she came in contact with.

Father Cholenec and Father Chauchetiere had been reciting the prayers for the dying in Kateri's last moments. Most people present seemed transfixed, unable to move away. All attention was drawn to their blessed friend's face. Father Chauchetiere watched Kateri's countenance with astonishment, as did all the others present. After a little while, her face became instantly beautiful. The scars from small pox she had worn all her life suddenly disappeared and her skin became flawless. The people, Kateri's people, gasped. This child of the woods, this beautiful flower belonged to them.

Anastasia, recalling the horrible small pox epidemic that took place so many years ago, looked upon Kateri and exclaimed, "Little Sunshine!"

Before the people left the cabin, they filed passed Kateri's body. They desired to touch her hand, and gently stroke her cheek. They felt as if by doing so they might bring their own soul closer to God.

When everyone had left, Therese, Enita, and Anastasia prepared Kateri for burial. They combed, oiled and braided her hair. They washed her body and put on new garments. They put new moccasins on her feet and laid her upon a fresh mat. Again the visitors came.

Two Frenchmen arrived in the village and looked upon Kateri. They had remembered her from other visits to the Sault. To them she was the Indian girl who lived like a nun. But seeing her now in such a beautiful state was almost beyond their comprehension. One of them said, "This Christian heroine must be buried in the manner of our own nuns. We'll build a coffin for this blessed girl, the flower of the forest, this Lily of the Mohawks!"

And so it was that on Thursday afternoon of Holy Week, Kateri Tekakwitha was tenderly placed in a coffin and lowered into her grave. The site was one she had once chosen for herself. It was the spot beneath the tall cross near the river. This cross had impressed her when she first arrived at the Praying Castle. At the foot of this cross she had so often come to pray.

Author's Note

In all likelihood Kateri Tekakwitha will eventually be canonized and take her place among the saints of the Roman Catholic Church. She was born at Ossernenon, (Auriesville, New York), in 1656. Her father was a Mohawk chief, her mother an Algonquin slave. Tekakwitha lived an exemplary Christian life even before she became a Christian. Her virtue was well-known among her people and among the French who came to inhabit the New World. They brought word of her sanctity to Europe. She served as an example during the time she lived and she continues to do so today. Many miracles have been attributed to Kateri Tekakwitha and many people pray to her.

She was buried beneath the cross of the Mission du Sault, the Praying Castle, which was a haven for the new Christians of her time. The monument to Tekakwitha reads: *Onkew Onwe-ice Katsitsiio Teiotsitsianekarom,* (Kateri Tekakwitha, the most beautiful flower that bloomed among the Indians).

But she does not rest there. Part of her remains were interred in the chapel at the Praying Castle. The village was later called the new Caughnawaga. The chapel was destroyed by fire. The remaining precious relics of Kateri Tekakwitha now reside in Kanawake, Quebec, Canada. Pope Pius XII declared her venerable January 3, 1943. She was beatified by Pope John Paul II on June 22, 1980. Many people, especially our Native Americans, look forward to the day when she will be canonized a saint by the Roman Catholic Church.

Bibliography

Barthel, Manuel, *The Jesuits, History and Legends of the Society of Jesus*, New York, 1984.

Bechard, S.J., *The Original Caughnawaga Indians*, Montreal, Canada, 1976.

Bruehle, Marie C., *Kateri of the Mohawks*, New York, 1962.

Costain, Thomas B., *The White and the Gold*, New York, 1954.

Dorland, Arthur G., *Our Canada*, Montreal, Canada, 1949.

Grassmann, Thomas, *The Mohawk Indians and their Valley*, Schenectedy, 1969.

Mitchell, David, *The Jesuits—A History*, New York, 1981.

Morgan, Louis H., *League of the Iroquois*, New York, 1954; 2 vols.

Parkman, Francis, *The Jesuits in North America*, Boston, 1867.

Walworth, Ellen H., *Kateri Tekakwitha*, Buffalo, 1893.

Weiser, Francis X., *Kateri Tekakwitha*, Montreal, Canada, 1971.

Glossary

Areskoui—the god of war

Cascades—rapids or falls

Fort Orange—present day city of Albany, New York

Gan-a-shote—a dance that was performed without a partner

Gan-a-sote—bark house

Hiawatha—a great Iroquois chief whom the Mohawks claimed as their own

Ho-de-no-sau-nee—the people of the long house, the Iroquois

La Prarie—a town in Canada which housed the early Christian Indians

Iroquois—Indians who composed the Five Great Nations: the Onondagas, Oniedas, Senecas, Cayugas, and Mohawks

The League—the Five Great Nations united to govern the tribes; this system of government greatly influenced our own American government

Okis—evil spirits

Orenda—a code for the Iroquois to live by

Ossernenon—the Mohawk town where Blessed Kateri was born

Palisade—rows of poles constructed as a stockade to wall off towns for protection

Rakeni—blackrobes or blackgowns; the French priests of the Jesuit order

Rawanniio—the one true God; the God the Jesuit fathers brought to the Indians

Sagamite—ground corn mixed with liquid, a staple food of the Indians

Sault—rapids or falls

Shaman—a tribal medicine man or wizard

Ville Marie—Montreal, Canada, an early French settlement

Wampum—strings of small white or purple shells. With the coming of the white man, the beads were often made of glass. They represented peace, storytelling and tribal history. They were also used as decorations or money

BOOKS & MEDIA

The Daughters of St. Paul operate book and media centers at the following addresses. Visit, call or write the one nearest you today, or find us on the World Wide Web, www.pauline.org

CALIFORNIA
3908 Sepulveda Blvd., Culver City, CA 90230; 310-397-8676
5945 Balboa Ave., San Diego, CA 92111; 619-565-9181
46 Geary Street, San Francisco, CA 94108; 415-781-5180

FLORIDA
145 S.W. 107th Ave., Miami, FL 33174; 305-559-6715

HAWAII
1143 Bishop Street, Honolulu, HI 96813; 808-521-2731

ILLINOIS
172 North Michigan Ave., Chicago, IL 60601; 312-346-4228

LOUISIANA
4403 Veterans Memorial Blvd., Metairie, LA 70006; 504-887-7631

MASSACHUSETTS
Rte. 1, 885 Providence Hwy., Dedham, MA 02026; 781-326-5385

MISSOURI
9804 Watson Rd., St. Louis, MO 63126; 314-965-3512

NEW JERSEY
561 U.S. Route 1, Wick Plaza, Edison, NJ 08817; 732-572-1200

NEW YORK
150 East 52nd Street, New York, NY 10022; 212-754-1110
78 Fort Place, Staten Island, NY 10301; 718-447-5071

OHIO
2105 Ontario Street, Cleveland, OH 44115; 216-621-9427

PENNSYLVANIA
9171-A Roosevelt Blvd., Philadelphia, PA 19114; 215-676-9494

SOUTH CAROLINA
243 King Street, Charleston, SC 29401; 843-577-0175

TENNESSEE
4811 Poplar Ave., Memphis, TN 38117; 901-761-2987

TEXAS
114 Main Plaza, San Antonio, TX 78205; 210-224-8101

VIRGINIA
1025 King Street, Alexandria, VA 22314; 703-549-3806

CANADA
3022 Dufferin Street, Toronto, Ontario, Canada M6B 3T5; 416-781-9131
1155 Yonge Street, Toronto, Ontario, Canada M4T 1W2; 416-934-3440

¡Libros en español!